Ten Ways to Find Love
... and How to Keep It

Ten Ways to Find Love
. . . and How to Keep It

A Guide to Romance in the Digital World

Dr. Lisa Portolan

OPEN ROAD

INTEGRATED MEDIA
NEW YORK

Originally published in the UK by Echo Publishing, an imprint of Bonnier Books UK, London

ISBN: 979-8-3372-0539-7

This edition published in 2026 by Open Road Integrated Media, Inc.
180 Maiden Lane
New York, NY 10038
www.openroadmedia.com

To the loves of my life: Gino, Gigi, Pasquale, and Juno the dog

Contents

Contents

Ten Ways to Find Love
. . . and How to Keep It

Introduction

The search for love

There are certain human conditions that we all aim for—for example, happiness and love. Nobody wants to be unhappy, nor does anyone want to be loathed. As children, we may assume that when we grow up we will be happy, and we will be loved. It's only when we click into adulthood that it becomes painfully clear that these two conditions are not a constant, and indeed can be remarkably elusive on a daily basis.

Instead of thinking that perhaps we were duped, and consistent doses of happiness and love are *not part of the human condition*, we may conclude that there must be something wrong with us. That everyone else is capable of happiness and love, and we are the perverse, unlucky types who will spend the rest of our lives on prescription medications, *alone.*

But why do we think love is a requirement for a life well lived? A life with purpose. A real life. A realised life.

This is a question I have considered in depth, specifically as it relates to dating apps. I have a PhD on dating apps and intimacy. I conducted interviews and focus groups across a number of years examining why people joined dating apps, what they were looking for, how they presented themselves, how they interacted with others, and their levels of success in finding what they were looking for. I wrote 100,000 words on the topic, and you can find my thesis on the internet. You can also find the textbook I wrote on the topic, which is equally verbose. However, as a former journalist, I'm aware you can often summarise a tome into a snappy sentence. Here is my thesis condensed:

Everyone is looking for love

Like every tagline, this comes with multiple caveats. They are:

1. People join dating apps for multiple reasons. They might be looking for a relationship, a hook-up, validation, to alleviate boredom, or even to cheat on an existing partner (emotionally or physically). But alongside this rationale, all of my participants were also looking for love.
2. People are unsure whether a big love exists—and if it does, whether or not they are worthy of it.
3. The majority of people don't think a big love can be found on the internet, or in particular on a dating app. Sure, you can find a hook-up on a dating app, but *that person* needs to be announced by some sort of face-to-face experience.
4. People aren't looking for love all the time, but just sometimes, at certain pivotal moments in their lives.

Why do we search for love?

Participants in my research universally sought romantic love. These people ranged in age from nineteen to fifty (the age range was restricted for research purposes). Some had been married and divorced, others were in polyamorous relationships, some were single, and yet they all felt as though at this point in their lives they should have met the love of their lives, and the fact they hadn't signalled their failure as a human being.

Often they would point to someone else—for example, a family member—who had met their partner face to face, were now married with kids, had bought a home, while the participant was single, rented an apartment with a flatmate and stayed home eating instant noodles. This was the gist of many responses. Curiously, none of these people spared a thought for said siblings and their relationships: were they happy? Or did they too cry themselves to sleep at night, hoping, wishing, dreaming, in this instance, for singledom? A chance to go again, to start with a clean slate? To eat instant noodles and not clean up after other people!

Interestingly, the majority of my participants had other significant relationships in their lives—family, friends or even children—and yet the quest for *that person* continued. When asked the reason for their search, the responses could be distilled into two broad categories:

1. Humans are hard-wired to find romantic love.
2. Humans are conditioned to believe they need to find romantic love.

Some participants believed these categories weren't necessarily mutually exclusive; they could exist side-by-side.

There are large bodies of evidence which indicate that the capacity and desire for love is part of human evolution; that natural selection favours romantic love. It's notable that romantic love is unusual among mammals. Humans are also unusual in forming long-term relationships with unrelated individuals, like friendships. But humans and all other mammals share one kind of love: the bond between a mother and her offspring. The universality of this attachment suggests that it's the original, ancestral form of bonding—the first kind of love, from which all others evolved. Across millions of years, sophisticated forms of bonding have been observed through the fossil record, relating to packs, tribes and even couples, this last in particular related to caring for children.

Overall, according to my research, when it came to the search for love it seemed there was likely a component of nature *and* nurture. My participants were perhaps hardwired to want to find love (a code written into their DNA), but alongside this they were also conditioned by our culture to believe that they *needed* to find love—that without love, their lives simply hadn't started.

So it's not unreasonable to believe that there are forces, including natural ones, that propel us towards coupledom. But in our modern world, coupledom has a very specific look and feel.

The modern idea of love

Our current understanding of romantic love is fairly modern. The earliest recorded marriages in Mesopotamia, Greece, Rome, and among Hebrews were used to secure alliances and produce offspring. It wasn't until the Middle Ages that love began to be a real part of marriage. Only in the last 200 years has romantic love started to be perceived in the way we see it today, governed by a set of rituals and a series of milestones like engagement and marriage. This new idea of love brings together romantic part-nership, sexuality, identity, friendship and procreation. Many of my single research participants were waiting for this big love to set other life events in motion—things like buying property, and starting a family.

Anthony Giddens, the author of *The Transformation of Intimacy: Sexuality, Love, and Eroticism in Modern Societies*, believes that the rise of romantic love more or less coincided with the emergence of the novel. If we were to examine eighteenth century literature, including authors like Jane Austen and Charlotte Bronte, we see the rise of the novel in which love acts as a catalyst for the protagonists' stories. Though economics still plays its part: Elizabeth Bennett must find a husband of standing because otherwise her family might be plunged into financial oblivion; Bronte's Catherine doesn't marry the love of her life Heathcliff because he's not of sufficient social status, and instead enters a doomed relationship with a man of wealth, Linton. While these books might have been written 200 years ago, the same narrative elements are alive and well in modern day rom-coms, and in our expectations of a relationship today.

Modern times fuel our yearning for an all-encompassing, perhaps even unrealistic, love. Today we cling to the belief that we'll encounter the love of our life: someone attractive, intelligent, humorous, endlessly captivating, sexually adept, and always available. We harbour lofty expectations for this grand love affair, anticipating not only that it will ignite our lives and all their significant milestones, but also that we'll remain perpetually infatuated with our partner, casting an ongoing glow on our existence, making every day significantly brighter.

But it's unrealistic to expect one person to fulfill every role— companion, lover, intellectual equal, and emotional support— consistently. Pursuing such idealised expectations sets us up for inevitable disappointment.

In today's world, speed is paramount. We multitask on our phones, order food for quick delivery, and upgrade to the latest gadgets without hesitation. Even our approach to weight loss is about instant results, often resorting to designer drugs. This culture of immediacy extends to relationships, where intimacy is fleeting and disposable. We crave the best love, but demand it instantly, ready to discard if it fails to meet our expectations. Love is now a rolodex of readily available sexual and intimate partners, available through dating apps. Match with one, go on a couple of dates, discover a sexual dysfunction and move on. Match with another, have an extended chat online, decide they're boring and yell 'Next!' like a Broadway producer.

At the same time, we're searching for an ongoing love, a love that will last the length of our lives, a love which satisfies all our needs. As a result of this push-pull, this distressing tension between fast and slow love, we can find ourselves depressed, wounded, feeling less than, and potentially on the psychiatrist's couch describing our woes.

The modern idea of love comes with baggage. There is a pattern which we are expected to follow. The romantic narrative might include the meet cute, a period of modern courtship (with rules about how and where to date, when to have sex, how to announce the relationship on social media, when to introduce friends and family), a diamond ring, a wedding, a home, children, and so on. (For those who argue that this is a largely heterosexual narrative, the success of the push for marriage equality in Australia would suggest otherwise.) But those whose romantic lives don't follow this pattern might feel they have done things out of order, or incorrectly. Social media provided a steady source of romantic blueprints.

While some of my participants may have felt inadequate or like failures due to their single status, having not met the supposed fundamental requirement of finding love, others may suddenly realise the dream doesn't align with their desires.

Perhaps they never envisioned themselves in a traditional wedding dress, opting instead for a tuxedo, or they may prefer a polyamorous relationship, or realise they never actually wanted children.

This sudden revelation can be jolting, prompting participants to question their worth and validity as individuals. They were led to believe that certain milestones should define their happiness and purpose. But what if they don't? What if following this prescribed path only leads to misery? Instead of blaming the flawed romantic narrative they've been fed, people can assume it means there's something wrong with them. This internal conflict may manifest in destructive behaviours such as cheating, gambling, substance abuse, or simply despising their daily existence. Why? Because acting out is easier than confronting the reality that their desires don't align with societal norms, and that their version of happiness diverges from the conventional narrative.

Modern love and consumer culture

Our society is characterised by consumer culture. We are constantly being urged to buy the new thing and discard the old. There's a focus on the joy—the fleeting joy—of the *new*.

People scour malls on the weekend to buy new things they never knew they wanted or needed. They become obsessed with buying the latest phone or car, believing they must have the new colour, or the new gadget. Embedded in this idea is the notion that the new is better than the old; that the old is defunct, unnecessary.

We come to be defined by the products we buy and consume: the outfit we're wearing, the gadget in our hand, the shoes on our feet, the products in the overflowing house we live in. We become enamoured with Instagram influencers and try to repli-cate their designer living room or summer wardrobe. If we don't have those things, we won't be happy; we also will be defunct. Leave the consumption merry-go-round and you too are out.

Our attitude to relationships, love and intimacy are similar. We swipe through endless profiles of people, consuming poten-tial matches. We go on two or three dates per week, conscious that there will always be another date, another match, and likely the grass will always be greener on the other side. We choose a spouse, but even as we're walking down the aisle we can't help but wonder: was this the right choice? Could there be someone better out there that I've not yet met? In signing this marriage certificate, am I also signing away years of my life that could have been spent with someone else?

We're constantly second-guessing our relationship choices: one foot in, one foot out. Desiring commitment, desiring 'the one', a lifetime of love, and yet not utterly convinced that we've selected the right option. Because there are too many options! Consumer culture teaches us that there are a range of different colours and sizes—and wait! It also comes in strawberry flavour! How to choose? It also tells us that we can quickly discard the strawberry and move on to the peach or raspberry one.

It is the finality of the decision, the 'I choose you', which we specifically object to, because we dither, knowing that our options have narrowed—to one.

Had we been born in a different time, this selection would usually have been made for us, and we would simply have made do. And while this is problematic, particularly for those who were bound to someone particularly unpleasant, it also means that the constant dithering would have been avoided, and the 'make do' element would have kicked into gear.

We tend to seek soluble bonds. While we desire commitment,

that big love, we're constantly tying our relationship bonds loosely so we can quickly unravel them when the next opportunity arises. We love the fanfare (and the consumption) of the wedding, and everything it might signify, but we don't love the continuation part: the 'ever after' is problematic. We would prefer to discard and move forward, and consume the next, and the next, and the next, in an endless loop of romantic consumption.

The modern focus on the individual

The individual wasn't always the centre of all things. Historically, across multiple cultures, the family was viewed as the essential unit in society.

The decline of religion, politics, the rise of consumption and other factors, all compounded no doubt by technology and social media, have seen the rise of the individual, with the focus now on individual achievement, individual merit. Limitless ambition is rewarded.

Our ability to compromise for the greater good, for the team, the relationship, the family, has been compromised. If we do compromise, we may find ourselves keeping a mental tally, wondering when our needs will be met, and when the tally will be equal again. We give to receive, rather than just giving to give, and this affects our relationships.

The 'meet cute'

One part of the modern love story people have come to think of as essential is the 'meet cute', in which the protagonists meet in a strange, quirky or unique way—think of Bridget Jones's first encounter with Mark Darcy, while he's wearing a ludicrous Christmas jumper. The majority of participants, when asked about how they thought they should meet their significant other, fell into sappy, humorous anecdotes. Shouldn't I trip over their dog in a park? Or maybe I'll meet her on the bus, only to notice she's wearing the same scarf as me? This 'meet cute' blueprint was originally found in romcoms, and is now increasingly seen in social media, which provides a virtual handbook on how to live life, identity and, importantly, love.

At heart, we're storytellers, and most of my research participants thought a big love needed a *big story* to herald its arrival—something they could tell friends, kids and grandkids in the future, and of course post on social media. And for most, meeting someone on a dating app just doesn't have the same type of cache.

Yet my participants also thought they *couldn't* meet someone face-to-face: that their hands were tied, and their only option was to meet someone in a tech-environment.

Why couldn't they meet someone face-to-face? There were two main reasons given. On the one hand, participants argued that people don't meet face to face anymore. They were always on their phone, swiping, DMing, updating their statuses. So even if you were eyes wide open, waiting to bump into Joe Black at the cafe around the corner from your house, Joe Black would likely be looking at his phone and not making eye contact. On the other hand, they believed themselves to be unworthy of this special kind of love, or this unique kind of meeting. The meet cute was reserved for uber attractive, intelligent and charismatic people. Participants would often lament, 'I'd love to meet someone face-to-face, but I'm not Jennifer Lopez/Emma Stone.' The conclusion was: they were the kind of person who could only meet someone on a dating app, the place where the rest of the ordinary, run-of-the-mill people congregated.

Dating apps for hook-ups, but not for love

A lot of research shows that the stigma around meeting a partner on a dating app is long gone, and it's a fact that the majority of the single population frequently uses dating apps. Nonetheless, my research showed that participants were happy to find a hook-up on a dating app, but not the love of their life, for which they believed they needed that face-to-face meet cute.

When examiners read my PhD, they wondered whether it was only women who were looking for the magical narrative of a rom-com flick. You might also be wondering whether it was a uniquely heterosexual yearning. It turned out to be neither—men in my sample sought love, and would have preferred a meet cute, and LGBTQIA+ participants did too. It was a universal desire.

Participants rejected the sterile, digital landscape of the dating app; they craved the organic connection. They often used phrases like, 'You find love when you're not looking for it.' As a result, they covertly rejected dating apps (despite spending hours per day on them!). Dating apps were seen as the exact opposite of organic; they were strategic, measured, premeditated. They flew in the face of every romantic rule participants had been programmed to believe was required to find love.

Meanwhile, participants 'kept their numbers high' (swiped and matched with as many people as possible), maintained multiple direct message (DM) chats (refusing to overinvest in the one person), and played a steady game of return on investment (ROI)—which curiously fed into their sense that dating apps couldn't deliver an organic love story.

Overall, in maintaining their numbers, participants missed

out on a crucial step in intimacy: sharing—which I'll talk more about later. They never shared the details of their daily lives with individuals they met on dating apps because they were talking to multiple people at the same time, and this precluded them from developing a deeper intimacy with one person. It didn't occur to them that they had to actually put their eggs in *one* basket—had to take a risk on one person—to develop intimacy, or to fall in love. The very way they used dating apps meant they couldn't actually reach their desired objective.

The majority of my participants said there was just something missing on dating apps—you couldn't translate the essence of a person via a bunch of zeros and ones. Many said they couldn't get a sense of the quirks, the nuances of the person on the other end. What did they sound like? Smell like? How did they laugh? Did they use their hands when they talked? It was this kind of uniqueness which couldn't be transmitted online, and ultimately this was the kind of stuff people believed made up intimacy.

The inner child

Overall, we are tiny, grown-up children. We may have lived extra decades, decoded the ways of the world, learnt the rites of passage, participated effectively (for the most part, or enough) in society, but deep down we are still those very children we were a long time ago. The little girl who was told her sister was prettier; the boy who was not cuddled enough by his mother; the ones who witnessed toxic relationships in their homes, to a lesser or greater extent.

This is not so much of our times—we were always tiny, grown-up children, even in the Middle Ages, only nobody had stopped to dissect this phenomenon and come up with a name for it. Nobody told us that we entered dysfunctional relationships and acted in dysfunctional ways because of the slings and arrows inflicted on us as children. We are now aware that other people can be narcissists, or that we could be narcissists, or emotionally unavailable, or toxic. And somehow we have to find a way to move forward.

Finding love . . . and keeping it

In describing how our times affect the ways we think of, and search for, love I've tried to outline some of the impediments that might prevent us from meeting and keeping the loves of our lives. This is not to say that we're all doomed, and should give up the search. But knowing what we're up against is half the battle.

And once you've found love, the next obvious question is: how to keep it? Anyone who has been in a long-term relationship (or indeed any relationship) will agree the latter is the toughest element.

Australia has one of the highest life expectancies in the world (83.2 years on average, according to the latest research conducted by the OECD in 2021). Is it realistic to assume we can keep that big love across four, five or even six decades? Particularly when we expect them to be a life partner, best friend, sexual companion, shoulder to cry on, our intellectual and physical equal, and (in many cases) a diligent co-parent.

So how do people keep this big love going? I interviewed many couples who have spent a lifetime together and still look lovingly into each other's eyes, and I also interviewed those who had failed, to gather their insights and lessons.

The thing is, we're never taught the science of loving: we're just expected to know it. In addition, our society doesn't celebrate the cultivation, the nurturing of love—it just tells us we have to find it . . . which means we often get stuck on the finding (the new), rather than the rest of the story. I myself have fallen victim to that story, chasing love without being able to cultivate, nurture or retain it. After all, we've been sold the fairytale, which relates to the butterflies, first kisses, chemistry, sparks, passion . . . The rest is a mystery, and it certainly doesn't look like fun. It looks more like work! Ironically, existing alongside the search for newness is the desire to be married or in a long-term partnership, and we feel a failure if we're not. How do we resolve these tensions?

In this book I have synthesised the research data from surveys and interviews into the ten top ways of finding love (according to hundreds of research participants), giving background as to why these strategies are likely to deliver on that big love. Then I list the top ten ways of keeping that love alive—again, using data gathered from my research. Peppered throughout are case studies from my participants.

In crunching data to distil the ten ways of finding love and keeping it in a scientific fashion, it wasn't lost on me that I was applying business principles to this ephemeral, intangible emotion, looking for a formula for magic—which by definition is impossible. In conducting my research I read the work of theorists, scholars and academics from sociology, psychology and beyond. However, I'm aware that there are elements to love and the maintenance of love which are unquantifiable— the kind of kismet stuff which has led people to be fascinated by love for centuries. I acknowledge that love can't be solved equation-style—but this is as close as I can take you (magic is sold separately).

♥ Case study: Rose

Waiting to meet someone . . . and for life to begin

Rose is thirty. She lives in Clovelly, Sydney, in a share house. She has two flatmates, both single women of a similar age. She has a degree in communications and a master's degree in public policy. She grew up in Canberra and in her mid-twenties left Canberra and headed to the promised land—the bright lights, glitz and glamour of Sydney. She began working at an advertising agency, and entered a world of frenetic busyness, where someone's importance is judged by how many events they have in their social diary. Make yourself too available and it becomes quickly obvious that you're a nobody—or so she says.

'Canberra was a nice place . . . quiet, though. The type of place where you could bring up a family. I didn't want that, or at least I didn't want that at that point in time. I wanted something more,' Rose said.

'I have this strange feeling, always, that my life has never really started. I'm thirty years old, and I still feel like I'm in this preliminary stage, waiting for my life to kick off. Perhaps I thought things would start . . . when I got here. But I still feel, well . . . not realised, I guess.'

Rose is incredibly articulate, with the ability to put complex thoughts into relatable language. She connects with the listener quickly. And she's an extrovert—a powerful characteristic in a world fundamentally made for the right type of extrovert.

'I have seven brothers and sisters—you know, a very Catholic family. I'm the youngest. My brothers and sisters are all in relationships. They're either married or they have partners . . . Most of them have kids and homes and important jobs. You know, they have actual lives. I'm not quite there yet. I'm still waiting for that to happen.'

For all intents and purposes, Rose would seem to have it all together. She's highly educated, works in a big advertising agency, in a high-profile job, and lives in an affluent and incredibly beautiful part of the world.

I ask her why she feels like she hasn't made it, or her life hasn't started, or why her life isn't as worthy as those of her brother and sisters. Like most people, she doesn't respond to the question directly, but her answer signals a larger internal conflict—the feeling behind the response.

'You see, I don't really like my job. Bizarrely, it was kind of my dream job. When I studied communications, working in a big advertising agency in Sydney with huge brands—that was my dream. But now that I'm doing it, I work really long hours, I'm constantly anxious, under pressure—and I feel like I'm doing meaningless work.

'I don't like my job; I don't own my home—I rent my place with a couple of other girls. I'll never own a home, the way things are going in Sydney . . . and, you know, I haven't met someone. I'm not in a relationship.'

'Do you think if you had met someone it would feel different?'

'Yeah, I suppose . . . Sometimes I think if you don't meet the love of your life, it's kind of like your life hasn't started. And then other times I think . . . who cares? So what if I don't meet someone? I have great friends. A fulfilling life. You know?'

I nod—even though this contradicts what she has just said. But this contradiction is common with my participants:

a sense of love-urgency, followed by ambivalence. It's like they don't know which camp to sit in, and society is telling them to sit in both, but it's impossible to straddle the two.

'Maybe if one of those things was in place then I would feel more . . .' She searches for the right word, and then says, 'I don't know.'

'And is that why you're on a dating app?' I ask, bringing it back to the research.

'I suppose.'

'So, you're on the apps to meet the love of your life?'

'No!' she scoffs. 'I mean, sure, if I meet someone on the apps then that would be great . . . but I wouldn't say that's *why* I'm on the apps.'

'So, why *are* you on the apps?'

'I guess for a bit of fun . . . Mostly to relieve the boredom. You know, a bit of chitchat or whatever . . . I started using the apps when I was living in Canberra. In my early twenties . . . Just because everyone was using them. But Canberra's a small place and you kind of know everyone there . . . so it didn't really work. I probably really started using them when I got to Sydney—you know, to meet new people as well.'

'And what apps do you use?'

'I started with Tinder, but it felt like it had had its day, and then Bumble, but I rarely got any responses on Bumble. And now Hinge, because it's more of a relationship app.'

'So you didn't have any luck on Bumble?'

'Nope! I'd message guys and they'd never message back.'

'Because women have to message first on Bumble, right?'

'Yeah . . . that's right. Don't get me wrong, I'd usually let guys make the first move, but on Bumble you have to, and I would literally get no responses.'

'That's interesting—you'd usually let guys start the chat on apps?'

'Yeah—I guess I'm a bit traditional like that. I think men should make the first move. But on Bumble you have to—and yeah, nothing.'

'Why, do you think?'

Long pause.

'I don't know. Maybe deep down men find it a bit intimidating when a woman makes the first move.'

'Even today?'

'Yeah . . . I think so.'

'Okay—so you said you're on Hinge now because you said it's a relationship app, but before you said you're not really looking for a relationship.'

'I'm not really the hook-up type. I am looking for a relationship—but I just can't imagine finding it on an app. I know that's a funny thing to say, and everyone's like, apps are the place to meet someone . . . but it just seems so wrong to me.'

'What feels wrong about it?'

'I don't know . . . I guess my brothers and sisters all met people face-to-face. Why am I the only sibling that has to meet someone on a dating app?'

'Do you think you should meet someone face-to-face?'

'Yeah, I guess. I mean, you grow up watching all of these romantic comedies, and thinking your eyes are going to meet someone's across a room sort of thing—and that just never happens. I feel like I'm a bit of an old school romantic. My parents were high school sweethearts; they met when they were sixteen at school, and then they've had this incredible relationship . . . They've built this family together. I was spoiled in that way—I thought something similar would happen to me, and then, well, it didn't.'

'And dating apps are a poor substitute?'

'Exactly! People are like—nobody meets face-to-face anymore, you need to be on a dating app, but I just feel like it's so desperate and strange.'

'What makes it strange?'

'It's like people are compressed in this strange way—into a couple of images and a bio—and you're supposed to make a call on that . . . and somehow it makes you incredibly judgemental. I look at men's profiles and if they're not tall, dark and handsome, I'm like, nup, you're out. Next!'

'So it makes you judgemental? You wouldn't act like that in real life?'

'Absolutely not! You know, when you meet people in real life, you hear the tone of their voice, the sound of their laugh . . . all those little bits and pieces that make someone . . . someone, I guess.'

'So what has your experience been like on Hinge?'

'Not great.'

'How so?'

'Well . . . at first it was like Bumble. I was getting virtu- ally no matches, no direct messages. I'm there thinking, I'm a good-looking woman, with an education, a great job . . . what's this about?'

'So what happened?'

'Well, I ended up showing my profile to some of my friends and they were like . . . you look super high-maintenance. You're way more chill. You need to fix this.'

'Interesting. So what made your first profile high- maintenance?'

'I had all of these photos up of me going out . . . you know, dressed up, make-up done, hair done, that sort of thing. And I do like going out. So I don't think it was a bad representation of myself. Also . . . I think I only take photos when I'm out . . . it's not like I take photos of myself when I'm working out, or relaxing at home, you know?'

'So it was just the photos that made you high-maintenance?'

'Yeah. And in my bio I had "Living a champagne life on a beer budget" . . . and my friends were like, that has to go.'

'What was wrong with that?'

She laughs. 'I don't know! I thought it was funny. And I thought it was very true as well! But they thought it might convey that I was high-maintenance! Which I'm absolutely not . . . I'd also put down that I had a master's, and they said to get rid of that—makes you seem stuck up, and too smart.'

'Okay . . . so too smart is also high-maintenance?'

'Well, I don't know if it's high-maintenance—but I guess it's intimidating.'

'Which is a problem?'

'I suppose.'

'So what happened?'

'Well, I changed my profile. I added photos of me hiking in Canada, no make-up, and some of me at home, and left one "done-up" pic, and I changed my bio to a quote from that *Liar Liar* movie, with Jim Carrey in it, something about the pen always being blue . . . And I started getting matches and chats.'

'Why did you use that quote?'

'I remembered that my brothers liked it, and thought it would be the type of humour that appealed to men. Or made me seem, you know, chill and cool. The type of girl who cracks jokes and watches the footie.'

'You don't like the movie?'

'No . . . never watched it.'

'So then you start getting matches once you changed your profile shots and bio.'

'Yeah. At the start of the year my phone was pinging off the hook with notifications from dating apps.'

'Did you feel a bit weird about needing to represent yourself in a different way to get matches?'

'I guess, but it's such an artificial environment. It feels like a bit of a game, so I didn't feel too weird about it. It's not like that's how I am in real life or anything.'

'I see . . . so it's just to get more matches?'

'Yeah, I suppose.'

'And where to from there? Did any of them progress to dates or relationships?'

'Not really.' She laughs, and then looks sad. 'My phone was just going wild, to the point where I had to turn notifications off. So many matches and chats, I felt like it was a second job almost. Sometimes I felt so overwhelmed just going back to my phone and finding all those messages—I didn't know where to start.'

'Would you say that you felt anxious about it?'

'Absolutely It was kind of like that stress when you come back from a holiday and you have 15,000 emails in your inbox and you're like . . . I can't do this.'

'But nothing eventuated?'

'No. I mean, it's a bizarre experience. It's like the middle part of the experience is taken out. There is the original chitchat at the start of getting to know someone . . . and then there's sex. There's nothing in between. There's not that getting to know a person, like if you were meeting someone in the office, for example. It's just not . . . right.'

'But you don't use the apps for hook-ups?'

'No way—it's so off-brand for me . . . I'm more the serious relationship type. I went off the apps for a while because it was just stressing me out too much; it's such a time-waster, and I think it was making me feel more emotional about everything.'

'Why's that?'

'I'm 30, so this is a key year for me, in terms of moving things forward . . . A key year in terms of . . .'

'Meeting someone?' I fill in.

'Maybe. I don't know, maybe.'

'So you've had no interactions from a romantic perspective during this period?'

'No. After I went off the apps, I started texting with a guy I met last year and went on a date with. I met him on a dating app, and he was a bit older than me, in his forties, but still, you know, attractive, youngish. He'd never been married, no kids, worked in finance . . . He ticked all the boxes, but there was something creepy about him. I couldn't put my finger on it at the time. But then he started texting me . . . We were texting for ages, but then it got weird. He started saying things to me like "Can I come around and fuck?" Out of the blue, in the middle of the day. And I'm like . . . no. But then he got really insistent, and he was saying weird things like, "I'll brush your hair and then we will fuck." I ignored him, and he sent all this crazy stuff about how I'd never have sex ever again . . . So I ended up blocking him. It actually really creeped me out, because he had my address and everything, because he'd dropped me off after that first date.'

'You were scared he would come to your place?'

'Yes and no. I mean, I live with two other girls, so it's not like I'm alone, but it did creep me out a bit.'

'I can imagine. Did you think about reporting him?'

'I mean, to who, right?'

'So now where are you at with things romantically?'

'Well, I'm back on the apps. I do that all the time. I go on, nothing happens, I get frustrated, and then delete everything, and then I think . . . well, where am I going to meet someone now? And I go back on, and the cycle begins again. I haven't met anyone. But, you know, I have my flat-mates, we're like a family. And we support each other . . . We laugh and cry together; we commiserate. I don't know where to with men. Maybe I'm one of those people who'll never meet anyone. Maybe I'm just too difficult. Maybe I'm asking too much. Maybe other women would have entertained the brush and fuck idea? I don't know. I might just be too much.'

'You think you're too much in relationships?'

'Well, I've been told that before—I've been told that I'm high-maintenance.'

'And what does that mean?'

'I guess, that I want . . . that I want to be treated right. Like I should be. And, I suppose, in today's market that's just too much.'

PART ONE

Ten ways to find love

1

Date like you're on holidays

Be open to the possibilities

We're often told that *love finds you—you don't find love*. Finding love when you're *not* meticulously scouring the dating scene is a romantic idea that has inspired filmmakers and authors alike— and drawn a mental blueprint of what love should look like for the majority of us.

In the movie *Notting Hill* (1999), the affable Hugh Grant, playing the quintessential British bookseller, stumbles upon love in the form of Julia Roberts, a dazzling American actress—like stumbling upon a rare book in a dusty second-hand store. Then there's the beguiling *Serendipity* (2001), starring John Cusack and Kate Beckinsale, where two souls share a fleeting moment and decide to throw caution and phone numbers to the wind, letting destiny steer their romantic ship—love served with a side of cosmic coincidence. Richard Linklater's *Before Sunrise* (1995) dangles on the edge of the unexpected, as two strangers meet on a train and decide to ditch ordinary life for an evening in Vienna.

Jane Austen's timeless *Pride and Prejudice* (1813) proves that the art of surprise in matters of the heart is not confined to modern sensibilities. Elizabeth Bennet and Mr. Darcy ultimately find love where neither intended to look. In Elizabeth Gilbert's *Eat, Pray, Love* (2006), love takes centre stage amidst a journey of self-discovery.

The irony being that there is indeed a premeditated agenda: that *love will just happen to us*. We don't need to find love, or even to open ourselves up to the potential of finding love. Rom-coms, fiction and social media teach us that there is a blueprint for love, and anything outside of that blueprint is just not, well, love.

Love should be kismet, it should be magic, it should just happen. Looking for love is not just frowned upon, it's simply unheard of! Which means looking for love on a dating app is an exercise in futility.

The importance of openness

Because so many believed that love should find you, many of my respondents felt slightly uncomfortable, perhaps off kilter, about the entire dating app experience. The idea that they were looking for love meant that something about their romantic experience was awry.

When I asked my respondents why they used dating apps at all, many would say, 'I'm bored, I need the entertainment.' This kind of ambivalent response could be read in two ways:

1. We live in a digital age where we have to be constantly entertained. We need to be swiping on Tinder, ordering Uber Eats and binge-watching Netflix to feel alive.

2. Participants were going along with the idea that they were *not* looking for love. They weren't looking for love on dating apps! Absolutely not. They had simply downloaded Tinder because they were bored. Nothing to look at here, guys! The steady swipe, swipe of the finger on the screen was a reflection of one's apathetic mood towards the times, and life— not their need for love!

And perhaps for many it was a combination of the two. Participants would also say that they didn't think they could find love on a dating app, but not being there was akin to relationship suicide, because no one was meeting in person anymore.

This kind of negative thinking was a formula for disaster. Participants were setting up a situation for themselves in which dating apps couldn't possibly find them love, and this became a self-fulfilling prophecy.

One of my participants who routinely went on and off dating apps concluded, 'If there was someone out there right for me, they'd literally knock on my door. If it's meant to be, it's meant to be. They will find you!'

But will they find you? Are we waiting for the Uber Eats delivery person to be Harry Styles?

What is your 'type'?

Alongside this kind of negative thinking, people often had rigid ideas about the type of person they would consider being with. While the heart (according to contemporary ideas of love) may not be equipped with a checklist, research in psychology and sociology suggests that people are often seeking a partner with certain characteristics.

The search for a type has its roots in evolutionary psychology. It's a tale as old as time—individuals gravitating toward traits that, from an evolutionary standpoint, promise compatibility, reproductive success, and the perpetuation of the human species. Picture it as a survival-of-the-fittest dance, where preferences for certain qualities become the evolutionary beat.

Studies in the field have revealed that humans often seek partners who mirror familiar traits. Familiarity, it seems, breeds not just contempt but also affection. The comfort of the known, whether in terms of physical features, personality traits or shared interests, becomes a guiding star in the navigation of romantic pursuits.

The desire for what's familiar

The British author Alain de Botton has examined how the familiar can influence our choices in romantic relationships. He uses the concept of the 'love blueprint'—the patterns and behaviours people subconsciously absorb from their early experiences, particularly within their families. He notes that individuals often find themselves attracted to people who bear a resemblance to their parents, whether the familiar traits are nurturing and supportive or potentially toxic. This extended to physical elements, personality traits and beyond.

Sometimes it's a simple physical type that a person is unwilling to look beyond—for example, one of my research participants declared 'I like them tall, dark and handsome. If they're not six foot three, then I swipe right.'

This desire for the familiar or a type extended beyond traditional notions of attractiveness or what society would tell us is good-looking—for example, another participant said, 'I like the muso types. You know, with a bit of a dark sense of humour.'

Overall, there was a sense that people—male, female and non-binary—knew what they wanted and were unwilling to experiment outside of their types. Types could also be unusually specific and as a result difficult to find: a needle-in-a-haystack search.

Recently, I was interviewed on a radio station. I had a chat with the producer in advance about what topics we might discuss, but when I found myself live on air with the journalist, the discussion turned to dating sites like RSVP and eHarmony, neither of which were part of my research.

The questions related to the algorithms used to match people, and the 'special sauces' dating apps claim to have in matching such people. Both RSVP and eHarmony have long surveys where the individual describes who they are, who they are looking for and what type of relationship they're seeking. The algorithm then matches the individual with like-minded people. But the questions were about how the algorithm was getting it *wrong*. The interview included a talkback element, and one of the callers said, 'I'm an academic, looking for another academic, and I've indicated that in my survey, but the algorithm keeps throwing me people with no education. Men that work in construction, or athletes. What's that about? Does the algorithm even work?'

I explained that if you have only a small number of people using an app, the algorithm can only produce the closest match—which might not be that close. For example, if you were in remote or regional Australia using a dating app, and you were seeking an academic, the number of potential matches might be small—possibly non-existent. If you were living in a city, then critical mass would work in your favour, and you might be matched with someone with a similar profile.

'Could I just be matched with someone more appropriate to me?' the listener said.

'Can she?' the radio journalist asked me.

I explained again that the algorithm only works if there is a large group of people on the app—otherwise you'll be matched with someone who fits some of your criteria but not all of your criteria. But I added that there is something to be said for dating someone different, someone who might not be 'your type'. Being open to different possibilities.

Dating apps and types

The fact that we are attracted to the familiar can have both good and bad outcomes. The good: there can be commonality between the two parties—you may have shared values, similar interests and pursuits, a similar vision of the future and how the relationship should unfold. The bad: the seeker may also be looking for a carbon copy of a parent, who may have been nurturing or toxic. We can be attracted to the qualities that hurt us the most.

Have you ever had a friend who seems to be consistently attracted to dismissive types who can't offer that person the security they yearn for? Yet when said friend meets a steady, loving, available sort, they quickly reject them, claiming that there is no spark or chemistry? This chemistry or spark might indeed be camouflaging the familiar—that is, familiar traits from their childhood and the way they perceived love and relationships within their home.

This kind of desire for the familiar, for a type, for a similar relationship style, is reinforced by dating apps. When users fill out surveys describing themselves, their likes, dislikes and interests, and what type of person they would be interested in, they are served with profiles that meet these criteria. Though not always: sometimes there are simply not enough people on the app for you to meet your 'perfect match'.

Alongside this, dating apps use artificial intelligence (AI) to learn about your behaviours on the app. If you consistently swipe right on blonde women, the app will continue serving you these types of profiles, as it believes it to be your type. You're getting what you're looking for. But are you?

AI algorithms on dating apps use a combination of user preferences, behaviours and other data points to recommend potential matches. These algorithms aim to understand your preferences based on your swiping patterns, interactions and profile information. While the exact workings of each app's algorithm may vary, the general idea is to provide users with profiles that align with their preferences.

If you consistently swipe right on profiles with specific characteristics, interests or demographic factors, the AI may take note of these patterns and present you with profiles with similar traits. The goal is to enhance the likelihood of matching with people who align with your preferences, and improve the user experience. That said, no one knows a dating app's special sauce and some argue that the dating apps throttle appropriate matches so that users spend longer on the app, or buy the premium packages.

Date like you're on holidays

I asked my participants in long-term relationships: what would be their number one recommendation for finding love? The majority responded: being open. Responses included: *being open to the unexpected, being open to possibilities,* and even *date outside of your type.*

The overall message was that love can be found in many different places and with many different people, whether it be on a dating app, in the supermarket queue or with an old friend (even someone who had been friend-zoned long ago). Many said that the person they had fallen for was not their type; that this person might have different values to them, different perceptions of the world.

As one of my participants said:

> My partner and I are very different. I'm very ambitious, and he's not. He's very reserved, and I'm very extroverted. But there's something about unpacking him and understanding him. It's like I'm constantly discovering something new . . . I like the idea that we're so different. It means I'm constantly surprised and learning.

Another participant said he had met his own partner while travelling for work in Melbourne.

> I was down in Melbourne for work, and I thought—why not switch on Tinder and see who I can meet? Later that evening, I met him for a drink at a bar in Melbourne, and I just felt like I was on holidays. Like I was open to new people and new things and it was all so exciting. Like a summer fling sort of thing. Only turns out we got married and we've been together for nine years.

This idea stuck with me as a good way to avoid getting stuck on a type, or the familiar: date like you're on holiday.

Hear me out: travelling, with its new horizons and diverse experiences, often acts as a catalyst for serendipitous romantic encounters. Removed from their daily routines, people are more receptive to the unfamiliar, making them more open to the prospect of meeting a romantic interest.

The shared sense of adventure inherent in travel encourages people to step outside their comfort zones, and this willingness to embrace the unknown often extends to interpersonal connections, making chance encounters more profound and memorable. The absence of preconceived notions and the liberating effect of being in an unfamiliar place allow people to be more genuine and unfiltered. The nature of travel instils a sense of impermanence, so that people are more likely to seize the moment and forge connections in a way they might not in their everyday lives. The collision of diverse backgrounds and cultures can also create a unique chemistry, transcending geographical boundaries and fostering connections that resonate on a deeper level.

In essence, hearts are more receptive to the unexpected magic of love on the road.

We're not always on holidays. In fact, it is the exception rather than the rule. But the message here is to take the kind of verve, enthusiasm and openness you might experience on holidays into your dating life.

Embody the holiday spirit

'I don't have time to date. I work, I go to the gym, I have to meal prep, catch up with friends . . . There's a lot going on. I need someone to slide into my life.'

My participants often sought love, but a kind of *love lite*—love that won't disrupt their life. Even when they were not particularly content with their life, they were caught up in its routines and unwilling to shift into a different mode. Unwilling to risk a life less ordinary, where love might have a place.

It became clear that cultivating a holiday spirit might open their hearts to the unexpected.

You might ask: but how do I do that with everything else that's going on in my life?

Here are some possibilities: start by setting an intention

around living like you're on holidays. Multiple studies indicate that setting an intention goes a long way in terms of achieving an outcome. You might want to start adding something outside of your routine on a daily basis: wear a vibrant shirt, or that lipstick colour that always seemed too bold. Try a different meal, or attend a random class outside of your comfort zone. Challenge yourself to doing one thing in 'holiday mode' on a daily basis, including from a dating perspective. Swipe right outside of your type, or start a chat in a quirky way. Feel that jolt of life, and open yourself up to love.

Closing down possibilities, only dating certain 'types' or doing only what's familiar, will yield the same results as our past dating ventures. The only way to produce a different outcome is to be open to all possibilities.

♥ Case study: Aditi

'We never really had that discussion'

Aditi is twenty-one years old, studies media at university in the evenings and works full-time at an insurance company. She lives in an apartment in Redfern with a flatmate. She has a tight-knit circle of friends she has known since childhood.

She's not looking for love per se—she's looking for a *connection*. Whether that be friendship, or sex, or a relationship, she wants to *feel something* intimate with someone. She's keeping her options open.

She uses multiple apps (on and off) to meet with people, including Tinder, Bumble and Hinge.

'I would definitely prefer to meet people in real life, but people don't go out to *meet* people anymore. Like, you don't go out to meet someone. If you go to a bar in town with friends, everyone there is just on a dating app, swiping. People just don't approach you anymore. Or they don't approach people like me . . . Maybe if you looked like Jennifer Lopez they would, but not someone like me.'

'What do you mean, someone like you?'

'You know . . . I'm not your typical good-looking girl. I'm kind of big, and I'm not that pretty. Guys say they want someone more chill or relaxed, not someone high-maintenance, but really if they must choose between the good-looking girls and me, who are they going to go with? Not me, of course.' She laughs, seemingly comfortable (and uncomfortable) with this outcome.

'So tell me a bit about your profile.'

'Well, it's a mixture of photos of me at festivals and doing stuff, out with friends. I like music, so I want to get across that it's important to me. I guess I want to show that I *do* stuff. I'm not the kind of girl that's just doing her make-up and buying clothes or whatever; there's more to me.'

'And do you feel like the images you've chosen are accurate—do they describe you well?'

'Yeah, most of them show my best side, you know? I'm not always dressed up and going to a festival. My average look is a long T-shirt and jeans, but I'm not going to put those sorts of images up, right? You have to sell it a bit.'

'Okay, and what's your bio like?'

'Oh, the bio is the hardest part. I get nervous writing my bio, so I usually get my friends to write it for me. Something funny and offbeat, because I'm kind of quirky.'

'You trust your friends with that?'

'Yeah, more than myself!'

'And do you have a fair bit of success? Have you made some connections?'

'Yeah, I guess. Last year I met a guy online on Tinder. He was this skater, musician-type guy. My age. We started chatting online, and we talked for ages. We were constantly texting and sending each other memes and news stories and stuff. He was into music and festivals, and the same sort of comedy as me. He was different as well. With guys my age, it's so hard to get them to show interest. You have to work so hard. But he was up for a chat. He started discussions and stuff. So that was nice.'

'And then you met him in person?'

'Yeah. We met in person, about two weeks later. We went for a coffee, and I was so worried that I'd meet him and he wouldn't be the person I'd been talking to, which happens a lot. Or that . . . he would think that about me. But he was, like, exactly like I imagined. His appearance—but even the way he talked—was exactly how I imagined. The same phrases he used online. I really liked him.'

'And where did it go to from there?'

'We started hanging out and talking. We'd go out, and he'd stay at my place and I'd stay at his, and we'd chat online all day. We both kind of decided that we didn't want to be in a relationship, or we didn't want to label it or anything. But we really got along—and things progressed pretty quickly.'

'So you ended up in a relationship?'

'Well, here's the thing . . . I mean, we never really had that discussion, and I guess I thought we were seeing each other exclusively. Like, we spent a lot of time together. I remember for New Year's Eve, I stayed over at his house, and then his mum and I were making breakfast in the kitchen and stuff. I was kind of like part of his family . . . So I guess I didn't feel like I had to have that conversation.

'And then a couple of months ago, it went a bit weird. We

were seeing each other less, and then he stopped sending me so many messages . . . I could tell something was up. So I asked him. I said, you know, is something going on? And he said he was just super busy with work, and anxious and stuff. So, I left it—but it didn't get any better . . . And then, a couple of weeks later, he said to me that he had been talking to another girl at the same time as me, and that he had figured out he liked her better, and wanted to, you know, formally be in a relationship with her.

'I mean, what was I supposed to say? We'd never had that conversation—and at the start we'd sort of talked about seeing other people at the same time, so he'd not really done anything wrong. I guess I'd just never set up parameters around this, because I just assumed, you know?

'So then he changed his profile on Facebook to "in a relationship". Straight after the conversation. So I just blocked him and that was the end of that.'

'Did it upset you that it ended like that?'

'Yeah, absolutely. I was gutted. I spent weeks in bed, crying. I mean, I felt like we had a real connection, and he was just seeing other people. It had a real hit on my confidence, my self-esteem . . . I went off the apps for a period of time to get over it.'

'And now you're back?'

'Yeah, I'm back on. I sort of just went back on for sex, to be honest. I'm a fairly sexual person, so sometimes I just like to keep it to a flirtation, or even a hook-up.'

'And do you change your profile when you're looking for something more sexual?'

'Not really.'

'And how has that worked for you?'

'It's been mixed, to be honest. Lately it's been a bit of

a nightmare. I know a lot of the girls would say they don't want to send a nude or anything, but sometimes I enjoy a bit of sexting. But recently it's just been a bit . . . I don't know, gross.'

'What do you mean by that?'

'Well, you know, most guys you meet online ask you for a nude. Sometimes it's really early in the discussion . . . Out of the blue, they'll just want a nude, and it's out of context . . . and gross. And then they'll just send you their dick. Again, out of the blue. I'll be sitting on the bus and get a picture message on Snapchat or whatever, and it's a dick. It's so embarrassing. Then I have to block them. It's so disrespectful, but kind of like weird and accepted behaviour in the online space.'

'Do you ever take action around it?'

'Yeah, sometimes. Once I was chatting to a guy and he started sending me dick pics, and I figured out he was actually dating someone I knew—so I ended up taking a screen grab of the photo and pixelating it, and sharing it on my stories on Instagram to friends, and tagging his handle, so people knew he was a creep.'

'And are you online at the moment?'

'I mean, not now. I got tired of a lot of the behaviour, you know, so I went off. But no doubt I'll be back. Give me a couple of weeks, you know . . . it's like a cycle. I think I just have to regroup a bit and go back to it. My self-esteem's been battered. I know my friends would say, you've got to get out there, but you know, I'm just fairly tired and a little bit disturbed by the whole thing. So, yeah, I need a break— but I'll be back.'

2

Turf the little white lies

Aim to be authentic

Most of my participants who were in long-term relationships named authenticity, vulnerability and honesty as critical to finding love—but the majority of my participants did not lead with these qualities.

This is somewhat unsurprising. After all, navigating dating apps sometimes feels like going to a virtual masquerade ball. People, in their quest for love, often engage in a dance of digital diplomacy. The fear of judgement and the pursuit of an idealised self-image lead many to present curated personas—like Instagram filters for the soul.

Do not blame the humble dating app user! Users are up against a barrage of other people, and the dating format encourages them to showcase their most socially acceptable selves in an unprecedented dating market place. Quirks are Photoshopped out, and vulnerabilities are left on the cutting room floor.

The gamified nature of dating apps adds another layer,

transforming the quest for genuine connection into a strategic quest for swipes.

Authenticity, it seems, takes a backseat to performance, leaving users to wonder if they are courting a real connection or merely engaging in a choreographed dance of romantic illusion. My participants often described themselves as constantly performing on dating apps, which made for a shallow kind of environment that did not encourage real connection.

And many are not being completely honest. They might be in an unhappy or unsatisfying relationship, and checking to see what or who is out there. Some might be in varying kinds of 'situationships', and not open to finding love.

But this is not only true of dating apps—even in the face-to-face world people put their best foot forward when it comes to love, and are not always entirely truthful. After all, as individuals we are all deeply flawed, and embarrassed about these flaws. Over the years, we've been taught to present a version of ourselves that others will approve of.

So what does authenticity actually mean? What does honesty mean? What does vulnerability mean?

Authenticity/vulnerability

Being authentic is essentially about being true to yourself, embracing who you are without putting on a show or conforming to external expectations. It's about living in a way that reflects your genuine thoughts, feelings, and values, rather than presenting a carefully curated version of yourself tailored to please others.

Social media tends to encourage people to appear to be a certain type of person: think of the prevalence of the 'coquette girl'—a flirtatious woman, often wearing bows in her hair, pearls, blouses and ballet flats. Social media has a series of readily available personal brands which we can try on for size. Express yourself outside of one of these known brands or identities, and you might fear you'll find yourself out of the loop.

One of my participants said:

> I met this girl and I thought I was in love with her. She ticked all the right boxes for me. We were from the same cultural background. She was modest, attractive and she wanted to settle down and start a family. And that's what I thought I wanted. Then when we got married, I felt trapped . . . it wasn't at all what I wanted, and she wasn't who I wanted.
>
> Don't get me wrong: she was everything she had presented herself to be. I was the person that had lied . . . I'm a free spirit, I'm quite wild. I needed someone to meet me in that place. I was just pretending to be the person everyone wanted me to be . . .
>
> Do you know how it ended? I cheated on her. I was just desperate to get out . . . and I couldn't figure out another way . . . A decade later, I think: it was all my fault. I was pretending to be someone else. She was a lovely person—and I hurt her a lot, and I have to carry that burden. I just wasn't being authentic to myself.

Honesty

Participants often said they felt they couldn't say what they really wanted from a relationship, themselves or the other person because of fear of censure. This meant the relationship was dishonest from the outset.

Honesty is about speaking the truth without sugar-coating it or hiding behind vague language; sharing your thoughts and opinions sincerely, even if it means addressing uncomfortable topics or expressing unpopular views. It means being refreshingly upfront and transparent, not trying to play games or concealing what's really going on—no fancy filters or hidden agendas.

Digital white lies

The majority of my participants engaged in digital white lies. This started with their profile and carried through to the discussions they had with matches. Profiles were heavily curated to create a picture that might be attractive to a potential mate. This involved a series of pre-conceived ideas about what men and women (or non-binary people) liked.

Heterosexual and queer men often felt pressure to come across as 'masculine'. This might involve using photos which displayed their 'built' physiques, or even using certain filters to appear nominally attractive. They might seek to present themselves as socially outgoing (featured in pictures with friends), and accomplished (education and career-wise). Heterosexual women sought to portray themselves as stereotypically feminine but not overdone—that is, they tried not to seem 'high maintenance' while appearing natural, relatable, friendly, and to some degree non-threatening to men. This could be seen as problematic—yet another way for women to make themselves seem smaller in relation to men.

The term 'high-maintenance' is part of everyday speech, and usually refers to a woman who places a high value on her personal image, wants or needs. In the context of dating, it implies that the woman in question is too much hard work; an easier, more relatable mate would be preferred. Hidden behind this seemingly insignificant, even innocuous idea was something far more sinister: the multitude of ways in which women are expected to rein themselves in to appease men—not complaining, not demanding too much, not expressing needs, not having expectations for emotional openness or fulfilment. In effect, not making any of the demands which are necessary for an intimacy based on equality and mutuality. The 'high-maintenance' woman was thought of as too much to handle, which reinforced the stereotype that women should be quiet, subservient, opinion-less, and always amenable. That they shouldn't be difficult.

The digital white lies continued into the realm of online chit-chat and even meet-ups.

One participant said:

> I met this guy on a dating app, and we had this prolonged discussion online. I knew things were a little off because he kept disappearing. Like, he would respond to messages quickly, and then all of a sudden he would stop and I wouldn't hear from him for days. I put it down to him being busy, but I had this sense things were off. Then he teed up a couple of dates and then cancelled them . . . but then he made all these overtures about seeing him. We had this great date, and then we kissed, and he invited me back to his place—but I wasn't completely sold, I had this feeling . . . Anyway, after that date he ghosted me. So I did some investigative journalism, and I found him on social media. Turns out he's got a long-term girlfriend. Maybe they were going through some stuff and he thought he'd test the waters to see what was out there . . . but why? Why present your-self like that to someone like me, who is genuinely looking for love?

A history of romantic white lies

The theme of individuals telling little white lies to romantic interests has woven its way into countless books and movies, adding layers of complexity, humour and drama.

The film *Cyrano de Bergerac* (later modernised as *Roxanne*, featuring Steve Martin) provides a poignant example. Cyrano, a poetic and eloquent man with a prominent physical flaw, helps his handsome but less articulate friend Christian to woo Roxane. Deeply in love with Roxane himself, Cyrano agrees to ghostwrite letters for Christian. The film deftly explores the consequences of these romantic deceptions.

In Helen Fielding's novel *Bridget Jones's Diary* and its film adaptations, Bridget Jones navigates the pitfalls of modern dating while grappling with her own insecurities. Bridget often fabricates a more polished version of herself in her diary, showcasing the relatable tendency to present an idealised image to the world. The story humorously explores the consequences of these little white lies on Bridget's quest for love and self-acceptance.

In the film *10 Things I Hate About You*, a modern adaptation of Shakespeare's *The Taming of the Shrew*, the protagonist, Patrick Verona, is initially paid to woo the sharp-tongued Kat Stratford. As the story unfolds, Patrick's genuine feelings for Kat emerge, highlighting the transformative power of authenticity in romantic relationships.

These examples collectively underscore the enduring fascination with the interplay of honesty and deception in matters of the heart. Whether driven by societal expectations, comedic misunderstandings or more sinister motives, characters telling little white lies in the pursuit of romance reflect the intricate and often messy nature of human connection. Audiences are encouraged to reflect on the delicate balance between authenticity and the artful dance of concealment that accompanies the pursuit of love—but also provided with a blueprint for falling in love, one that clearly includes lies.

Do we believe that lies and love are somehow intrinsically

linked? Or perhaps that if we were to present ourselves honestly we would be unloveable?

What if the opposite were the case? In the *Seinfeld* episode tided 'The Opposite', George Costanza decides to follow the principle of doing the opposite of his instincts, believing that his life has been a series of failures due to his bad decision-making. He boldly approaches a woman, telling her he's an unemployed man, living at home with his parents. To his surprise and the audience's amusement, the woman responds positively. She says men are always trying to be someone else, and she appreciates this kind of honesty and authenticity—and the pair go on a date.

What do the experts say?

Many relationship experts see authenticity, vulnerability and honesty as fundamental to building meaningful and lasting connections, acting as the cornerstones of intimate relationships, and providing a solid framework for understanding, trust and emotional depth.

Alain de Botton says that authenticity allows individuals to be seen and accepted for who they truly are. It involves embracing one's vulnerabilities, quirks and imperfections, so that partners can connect on a profound and genuine level.

Therapist and relationship expert Esther Perel says that vulnerability is the willingness to expose one's true self, including fears, desires, and insecurities. She argues that vulnerability is the gateway to intimacy, as it requires openness and a genuine sharing of emotions. Through vulnerability, individuals invite their partners into their inner worlds, creating a space for mutual understanding and empathy. This shared vulnerability, Perel suggests, forms the bedrock of emotional connection and fosters a closeness that goes beyond surface-level interactions.

Authenticity provides the foundation for vulnerability, as individuals must first embrace their authentic selves before exposing their vulnerabilities to a partner. This, in turn, paves the way for honesty, and open and transparent communication within the relationship.

In building relationships, these qualities act as antidotes to the potential pitfalls of modern love, such as superficiality, communication barriers and emotional disconnection. Embracing authenticity allows individuals to move beyond societal expectations and connect on a more genuine level, fostering a relationship that is built on shared values and true compatibility.

What did the research participants say?

As noted earlier, the majority of respondents in long-term relationships said authenticity, vulnerability and honesty were exceptionally important to building an intimacy, or finding love. Many described having previously been led astray by a partner, or having led a partner astray, finding that little white lies, or just lies in general, led nowhere in terms of developing a relationship.

One participant said:

I once dated this girl—I was really into her. She was a little unavailable but I thought that was just everyday life getting in the way. All of sudden she became more available, and I took this as her becoming more invested in the relationship . . . but found out on the grapevine she had been dating someone else. When I confronted her about this, she said she had been 'talking to other people' but decided I was the one. I thought this was a huge lie, and a reflection of her disingenuous character. We broke up . . . I always think she could have been my person, but I hated the way it started. I couldn't get past it.

Other participants using dating apps to find love said they looked for something starkly genuine in a profile or when they were getting to know someone that identified this person as authentic.

One participant said:

I'm so sick of someone saying they have an online business. What type of online business is it? Send me the link so I can check. I would far prefer that someone tell me they're unemployed than come up with some sort of cool façade. Makes me feel sick—it's a real turnoff!

Ultimately, lies destroyed relationships, and fledgling intimacies, whereas authenticity, vulnerability and honesty can stoke the kindling, allowing that intimacy to grow.

♥ Case study: Kristina
The trouble with faking it

Kristina is a 30-year-old nurse who lives in Penrith. We're conducting this interview via Zoom and Kristina is sitting on her bed, beaming in via her laptop. She's wearing a loose black T-shirt and a beanie.

'I'm a bit of a self-confessed tomboy,' she says. 'I don't know if that's an outdated term . . . I'm assuming it is. I'm not really the cool type or anything.'

'What do you mean by tomboy?'

'Well, you know, I'm not a girly girl. My standard get-up

is jeans and some Connies. I don't do make-up, and I have a motorbike. I grew up with boys on a rural farm, so I'm a bit boyish. But I'm not a lesbian; everyone always thinks because you're a bit of a tomboy, you're a lesbian, but I'm very heterosexual.'

'Have you found yourself explaining that a lot?'

'Yeah . . . people just don't get it. I'm just a bit blokey, almost. But I'm not gay. It's been really tough from an identity perspective. I feel like I've constantly got this tension between being myself and then pretending to be more like a girl. It's been like that since I was a kid.'

'Tell me a bit about what dating apps you're using and why you're using them.'

'Well . . . up until my mid-twenties, I had no issues meeting men, even if I was a tomboy. I guess I was lucky that way. I always met them face-to-face, at school, at work, whatever . . . And I'd say they were long-term relationships. But some of them were a bit toxic. After my mid-twenties, I kind of felt like I had to work on myself first, and then get to the relationship side of things, and I did that. And then in my late twenties, I was like, hang on . . . I'm just not meeting anyone face-to-face anymore. In a short period of time, everyone went online, and I just had to adapt.'

'And what apps are you using now?'

'Mostly Hinge. I went on Bumble initially, but no-one was matching or responding, it was absolutely dead, so I went to Hinge. Tinder's just not my vibe, you know?'

'Do you think it's a bit more of a hook-up app?'

'Yeah, it's like the bro-app. I'm not really into that—I'm looking for a relationship.'

'And why do you think Bumble wasn't working for you?'

'I don't know . . . I mean, I think men find it weird when

you start the chat, even if that's how the app is made. Maybe it's a patriarchal thing where they feel affronted by women suddenly starting the chat, so they just don't respond . . . Also, it was before I changed my profile.'

'You changed your profile?'

'Yeah. When I started on dating apps, I was like, authentic. I put up some pics of me: me and my motorbike, me in Bali, me bungee-jumping—I'm an adventurous, free spirit type, and I like motorbikes. But it was literally crickets. So then I showed my mum my profile, and my mum and I have this odd bond. We're super close. She's a psychologist, and she's always giving me advice about this sort of stuff. She thinks I'm on the shelf and will end up a spinster . . . She said, you need to be more feminine in your profile, put up some pics of you in dresses—still looking natural, of course, but the more feminine side of things. I didn't want to initially, because I never look like that, but eventually I buckled. I change my profile to these cute images of me and reduced my bio to like a couple of words like nurse, star sign, and that's about it . . . Boom, I'm getting all these hits, all these DMs . . . The world suddenly changes.'

'And do you find that off putting?'

'Yes, of course! Because it's not me! And I think, do I really want to go on a date with someone who wants this type of girl?'

'What type of girl do you mean?'

'Oh, you know . . . this pretty, nicey-nicey type. Not high-maintenance or anything—like the girl-next-door . . . Makes me want to vomit in my mouth. And then disturb-ingly . . . I find myself acting like that girl in the chats, like I have half a brain, and they love it! It's actually a real mind-fuck.'

'So do you go on any dates with these people?'

'No. That's the thing. I can't be bothered—because I know it's fake, fake, fake. But in the background my mum's there telling me that my biological clock is ticking, and I need to secure a man ASAP or forever hold my peace, and I won't lie to you, it stresses me out . . . And I think, will I ever get my own life . . . Will it ever start?'

'Have you felt lonely?'

'Yeah, I guess . . . I have a housemate, who's my best friend. But she's met someone and they're always together, and it makes me feel like, am I ever going to have that? And then there's my mum in the background telling me the clock's ticking, and this ridiculous fake situation on the apps.'

'Have you ever thought about reversing your profile, going back to the original one?'

'No. I mean . . . it just doesn't work. I've been going on TikTok . . . I find there's a lot of guys there, the kind of guys I'm interested in, and it's less of a contrived environment. I might follow someone's reel and then drop them a message at some point. It's not that weird fake vibe and there's less focus on what I look like, because you can see more of my personality, if that makes sense.'

'Yeah, I see what you mean. And what type of guys are you interested in?'

'Well, I guess I like Aussie blokes.'

'What do you mean by that?'

'Well, you know, because I'm kind of tall and a tomboy, I like a bigger man, you know, with hair on his chest, a beard. Aussie humour, a bit of a larrikin. Someone that can go out and camp . . . I'm a camping type, not a hotel type of a girl, you know what I mean?'

'Yeah . . . So, overall, what do you make of dating apps?'

'Look, I'm going to be honest. I get that their function-ality is all around matching people, and hooking people up, but I think they do the opposite—it's almost like they split people apart. If you think about me, I've now got this fake dating app profile. I'm pretending to be someone, but to what end? I don't actually go on any dates from it. So I'm kind of just wasting time. And it's reinforcing this awful stereotype in my mind: that men only want certain types of women—basic, pretty, nice women. Not challenging women. Not smart women. Not free spirits, and definitely not tomboys. It's like I'm being forced into this shape, and I'm resisting all the way—but it's the only one that will get me the outcomes. What's on the other side of that? Being alone—and to be honest, I'm not okay with that.'

3

Sharing

A crucial building block in intimacy

For some people on the dating apps, there is no need for sharing. For example, several of my participants used dating apps only for hook-ups, and by this I mean casual sex. Two were married to each other and in a casual non-monogamous arrangement, and used dating apps to hook up with other people. Their bios described their relationship status, and said they were only on the apps for hook-ups. They never divulged any information about themselves beyond their first names.

'I don't want to go to dinner with them and talk about current affairs and my hobbies,' said one. 'There's no sharing around who I am, what I do, what I like, and vice versa—because that's more than sex.'

This was common to all of my participants seeking hook-ups. There was no sharing of personal details. Overall, there was a concern that sharing would lead to something more, whether it be what Mei described as 'catching feelings', or developing a broader and deeper intimacy.

But what if you're on the apps looking for love?

Sharing as central to love

Sharing information about ourselves allows us to build an intimacy; the deeper the sharing, the greater the intimacy. It allows us to let someone else into our idiosyncratic worlds, and in turn get a glimpse into their equally odd reality and history. It makes us feel less alone, and more united. We may discover that we have experiences in common, and that the things that we believe make us odd are not so odd at all.

Sharing can bind two people together. One of my participants said:

> My girlfriend used to have this odd little apartment in Surry Hills. It was awful—tiny, mouldy, smelly . . . disgusting. But it's one of my favourite places. We'd stay up late at night, sometimes all night, and just talk about all this weird stuff. About our childhoods, and our parents, and our dreams, and I'd impersonate people's voices . . . It was honestly some of the most beautiful moments of my life. That's when I first fell in love with her, and discovered her—and she discovered me.

Sharing and dating apps

Many of my participants complained that the relationships they forged in the digital domain were surface-level. Most said the discussions were boring and focused on the minutiae of everyday life. Participants complained about conversation starters like, 'Hey, how are you?' or 'What have you been up to today?', saying there was no depth; that the surface-level chit-chat meant nobody really stood out from the crowd, nobody was unique.

At the same time, as we've seen, participants were talking to multiple people at the same time, and so busy with chitchat they never added depth to their discussions or expressed themselves in more detail.

In addition, there was a *general fear around being vulnerable and sharing too much*. Many had been previously scammed by online tricksters, or by people in real life, and felt they needed to keep their guard up as a result. Mei, who we met earlier, is a good example. She and the tradie she met online traded stories about their childhood, exes and everything in-between. Then he ghosted her. She felt devastated and switched to a hook-up experiment in which she decided not to share anything about herself at all.

Online dating can be seen as a game of emotional poker, where each participant guards their cards closely, fearing that revealing too much too soon might result in losing the proverbial hand. They yearn for genuine connection, yet fear judgement and rejection.

Sharing in the modern world

As noted earlier, the modern world has shifted from a more communal ethos to celebrating individual achievement. This contributes to a culture where sharing is often viewed with scepticism, or seen as antithetical to personal success.

Because personal achievement is glorified and the accumulation of wealth is seen as a marker of success, individuals may be less inclined to share resources, experiences, or feelings for fear of appearing vulnerable or compromising their competitive edge. We may prioritise individual goals over communal well-being and, in this case, love. We may want to have the upper hand, want them to love us more than we love them. Having the upper hand means we're less likely to get hurt.

The market-driven mentality may mean relationships are seen as exchanges of goods or services rather than shared emotional connections. This may discourage genuine sharing, as people fear revealing too much of themselves could undermine their market value.

Sharing resources or seeking support may be perceived as a sign of weakness or dependency. This can also inhibit the natural inclination to share within relationships.

The reluctance to share may manifest in various ways, from guarded expressions of emotion to a hesitancy to pool resources or build towards a common future. Relationships may become transactional, with people calculating what they invest versus what they gain. This approach can prevent the authentic sharing of emotions, dreams and vulnerabilities, thereby eroding the foundations of intimacy and trust.

So how do we challenge this? Cultivating empathy, prioritising genuine connections over transactional exchanges, and embracing vulnerability as a strength rather than a weakness can serve as antidotes to our societal reluctance to share. By recognising the value of shared experiences, emotions and resources, we can foster a landscape in which love can flourish.

Feel the fear and do it anyway!

We might need to force ourselves to share: to put ourselves out there and be vulnerable. We may need to risk being hurt!

Feel the Fear and Do It Anyway is a self-help book by Susan Jeffers that encourages readers to overcome their fears and live a more fulfilling life. Published a couple of decades ago, its simple message has stuck with me over the years and seems particularly applicable to dating. Jeffers offers a practical approach to understanding fear, and techniques for managing it effectively. The book emphasises the idea that fear is a natural part of life, but doesn't have to hold us back from pursuing our goals and dreams.

Jeffers encourages readers to reframe their thoughts about fear, viewing it as a signal that they are stepping out of their comfort zones and growing as individuals. Today, we tend to either ignore fear or self-medicate against it, without understanding that a healthy amount of fear is probably part of the human experience.

Jeffers outlines strategies for confronting fear, such as using positive affirmations, visualising success, and taking small steps towards facing fears gradually. She also discusses the concept of 'no-lose decisions', where even if things don't go as planned there is still something to be gained from an experience. Sharing (appropriately) is one of those no-lose decisions, where you can be sure you've done the right thing.

Without sharing, there is no intimacy, connection or love. Sometimes we need to take the risk, and be vulnerable.

Sharing versus oversharing

I was asked to be part of a six-part radio series on love in your fifties, which focused on how to find love in this second part of your life, specifically given dating had changed so radically.

Many of the people who I interviewed in this age group had been in one long-term relationship, or several. Now, post break-up, they found themselves in a brave new world where people no longer met face to face or through mutual connections but via dating apps.

For many this was a revelation—a plethora of people readily available, one swipe away!—and they threw themselves into it. For others, the world of dating apps felt uncomfortable, even unsurmountable: they didn't know the rules of the game and were unsure if they wanted to learn them.

One guest on the program recounted how she waded through the dating app world with much distress, only to finally connect with a humorous man, first online and eventually face to face.

> We had an instant simpatico. He was easy to talk to and we shared a similar kind of cringe-worthy humour. After chatting for some time, we decided to meet up in person at a restaurant for dinner. I was incredibly excited. In fact, I had that spring in my step, the feeling that I was embarking on something fun . . . and I guess I hadn't felt like that in a while . . .
>
> For the first maybe twenty minutes, it was great. He was exactly as I'd anticipated. He looked like his pictures: tick. He sounded like the person I'd been texting. It all had promise, and I caught myself thinking that.
>
> And then—well, it took a turn for the worst. He started talking about his ex, which initially I thought was an indication of him sharing, connecting, but then it really got in-depth, and it descended into complaining about the custody arrangement, his non-existent relationship with his daughters, and then on to his job, and how he felt defeated by it . . . and really everything.
>
> By the end of the night I felt exhausted. It was the kind of rampant oversharing that sucks the life right out of you. The thing is, he thought we'd had a great time, and he kept calling me to talk, and he wanted to take it further—but I literally had to block

this person. It was too much! So you say sharing is important to building a relationship—but how much sharing? When does it become oversharing?

One would think the line between sharing and oversharing would be obvious to people; that on a date, the other person would take a pause, and perhaps ask his or her match a question. But the art of conversation has been lost (we'll get to this in more detail later), and as a result oversharing can be a real issue, in all generations, but particularly with older men, where there could be some—or a lot of—baggage in the mix.

A date is not a confessional! Share, and by all means use sharing to build a connection, but make sure you leave something to the imagination: after all, love is a delicate blend of the known and the unknown.

4

Kindness

A non-negotiable

I grew up with loving parents. They're still married—and have been married for forty years. When I see them together, I still see love: in the little glances, in their words . . . but their relationship was never perfect. They'd often have volatile arguments, and would threaten to leave. Sometimes they *would* leave. They'd say hurtful things to each other—they still do! So I guess kindness was never really part of my family's dynamic . . . and it wasn't until I was in my forties, and I started seeing a counsellor, that I discovered I could be an unkind person—and I could be unkind to the people I was dating, or had just met, even! And I realised nobody wants that. Everyone wants someone who is kind.

This quote, from one of my interview participants, struck me on multiple levels. First, the description of his parents' relationship as both volatile and unkind, but also loving, and the impact this might have had on his understanding of love; second, how contrasting things can be true at the same time, for example that there could be meanness (the opposite to kindness) and love in this relationship; and third, his astute realisation that kindness is important; that nobody wants to be with an unkind person.

Kindness, in fact, was named by many of my participants in long-term relationships as a key factor in finding love and maintaining it. To some degree this is surprising—in the modern world, the concept of kindness does not get much airtime. Children are taught to be kind in the playground, in the same way that they're taught to share, but as they grow up this is largely replaced by a desire to be cool, to appear nonchalant, angry, jaded. Kindness is perceived as a weakness that can be taken advantage of in a tough world.

And yet kindness is very much required in the forging of unions, in the story of love.

A short history of kindness

Kindness has not always been perceived as unnecessary: historically, the threads of kindness are woven through time, transcending cultural boundaries.

In ancient civilisations, kindness was intertwined with moral and ethical codes. In ancient China, the teachings of Confucius emphasised kindness as a cornerstone of virtuous living. Fast forward to medieval Europe, where chivalry involved a code of conduct steeped in kindness and gallantry. During the Renaissance, philosophers like John Locke and Jean-Jacques Rousseau explored the innate goodness of humanity, so that kindness came to be viewed as a fundamental aspect of human nature. In the nineteenth century, there was a surge of philanthropy and social reform movements, where people like Florence Nightingale and Elizabeth Fry embodied kindness through their dedication to healthcare and prison reform. The literature of the time celebrated characters like Charles Dickens's Tiny Tim, where kindness was seen as a virtue worth cherishing.

Even in the harsh landscape of the twentieth century, with its wars and political upheavals, acts of kindness emerged as beacons of hope. The tales of righteous individuals who risked their lives to save others during the Holocaust, or the generosity of nations in the aftermath of devastating conflicts, demonstrated that kindness could withstand the darkest chapters of history.

Now, in the digital age, kindness finds expression not only in face-to-face interactions but also in online communities rallying for social justice and empathy.

My interview participants said the word 'kindness' often seemed out of place in the vocabulary of adulthood. The corporate world, with its emphasis on competitiveness and efficiency, often sidelines kindness. However, the very essence of kindness, rooted in empathy and understanding, remains a timeless and universal force that can bridge gaps in communication and foster genuine connections.

Kindness and love

In love stories, kindness often emerges as the unsung hero. Forget grand gestures and dramatic declarations—kindness often quietly steals the spotlight. Across the globe, from the Arabian Nights to African folklore, tales of love echo with kindness. Aladdin's selfless acts for Princess Jasmine, or the African folktales where kindness becomes a bridge between disparate worlds, showcase the universal truth that love blossoms where kindness takes root.

In more contemporary love stories, kindness often takes

the form of everyday gestures. It's the comforting cup of coffee brought to a weary partner, the unexpected note of encouragement, or the simple act of listening without judgement. In the bustling streets of modern relationships, where the cacophony of daily life can drown out softer sentiments, kindness becomes the secret ingredient that keeps love resilient.

Ghosting in the digital world

I held a focus group in an old library in Sydney with around twenty participants. Most of them were twenty to thirty years of age. They were a mix of heterosexual and queer participants, as well as people seeking different relationship structures, for example monogamy, ethical non-monogamy, etc. They were Australians and internationals. In fact, their only common characteristic was that they were on dating apps, looking for love. The aim of the focus group was to surface new and interesting ideas, angles that I had previously not considered in relation to dating apps and intimacy. We ended up in a conversation about rudeness and ghosting.

Ghosting refers to the act of abruptly ending communication with someone without warning or explanation. This typically occurs after a period of initial interaction, whether through messaging, texting, or even after a few dates. Essentially, the person who is 'ghosting' disappears from the other person's life without any closure or resolution—like a ghost.

'The dating world is tough,' one woman said. 'People are just rude—and they don't give you a reason as to why they don't want to continue a discussion, or go on a date with you. They just disappear. They just ghost you.'

'Why do you think people ghost you?' I asked.

'Because it's easy. You don't need to explain yourself to

someone, and you'll never have to! There are thousands of people on apps . . . If you don't like someone for whatever reason, then you just move on, and that's it. *Next!'*

The group laughed.

'I think dating apps have made people more brutal,' a man in his mid-twenties declared.

'In what sense?'

'In the sense that someone says just one odd little thing in a chat, and you'll be like, nup, I'm out. Like it will be a small thing that you'd normally tolerate in the outside world, but on the app, you just hit the exit button.'

The group nodded again and there was some giggling. It appeared this was a common sentiment.

'Why do you think that is?' I asked.

'Because there's so many people on the dating app . . . I guess it starts to feel like a game. You lose a sense that . . . that . . . there's someone else on the other side. It doesn't feel real.'

The original speaker jumped in: 'Except when it happens to you!'

'That's true,' he conceded. 'It's hurtful when it happens to you. But that's part of it. You start thinking, well, I've been ghosted heaps of times. Why should I afford someone else an act of kindness? Nobody's done that to me.'

A twenty-one year old woman responded. 'Last week, I'd made plans to see this guy on Saturday night. We'd met on a dating app, and gone on one date. He seemed pretty nice. Maybe a little distant, but there was enough there to go on a second date, and we'd made this whole plan . . . An hour before we're supposed to go, I'm already ready. You know, I've had my hair blow-dried, done my nails, bought a new outfit . . . A girl has to get ready!'

The group nodded, understanding the preparative rituals required.

'. . . and then I get this text from him saying some friends of his have arrived from the UK out of the blue. He can't go.'

'I've heard that one before!' someone quipped.

And I think to myself,' she went on, 'who has friends that arrive from the UK randomly? Is this a lie? But because he's gone to the trouble of actually giving me some sort of excuse, I think to myself: give him the benefit of the doubt. Maybe it's true. Anyway, the next day I text him to check in on him—and I never hear from him. Ever. Again.'

The group laughed raucously, but there was something desperately sad about the sound as it echoed around the room.

'Like this is normal behaviour,' the woman continued. 'There's no courteousness or kindness—it's cut-throat.'

'Cut-throat,' someone echoed.

'Would you say ghosting has become a social norm?' I asked.

There was a chorus of 'Yes!' and 'Absolutely!'.

'Have you all ghosted someone?'

Participants nodded, with some titters of laughter.

'It's just not so nice when it happens to you.'

'It's kind of like . . . this is what you expect now. It's dog eat dog.'

This discussion highlighted for me the competitiveness underlying the modern search for love online, the alienation that is part of the digital domain, and ultimately the loss of kindness.

The old rules of courtship

Participants felt like courtship had disappeared, and with it courteousness, kindness and other social rituals which make dating pleasant. They thought this was a reflection of the times, and in particular the disposability the digital domain had encouraged: the swipe and flick mentality.

Many of my participants (particularly women) talked about a Jane-Austen-esque courtship and how these kinds of dating rules and pageantry had long disappeared. Today's world of dating was more akin to the digital wild west, replete with random requests to 'send nudes'.

In the real life 1800s, courtship was governed by strict conventions and rigid gender roles. In an era marked by formality and restraint, dating was often a family affair, with parents actively involved in selecting suitable matches for their offspring. Young men and women were expected to adhere to a set of prescribed behaviours, dictated by societal norms and often steeped in tradition. Chaperones often oversaw the couples, to ensure propriety and moral decorum. The emphasis was on the virtue of women and the gentlemanly conduct of men; the expression of romantic interest was *subtle and indirect.*

As the twentieth century dawned, a seismic shift occurred. The Roaring Twenties ushered in an era of rebellion against Victorian constraints, giving rise to the 'flapper' phenomenon. Young women, embodying new-found independence, embraced shorter hemlines, bobbed hair, and a bold attitude. Dating rituals became less formal, and the concept of 'going steady' gained traction, signifying a more exclusive commitment.

The mid-twentieth century saw the emergence of a dating culture that bears some resemblance to today's. The post–World War II period brought about increased mobility, economic prosperity, and a cultural shift towards individualism. Young people began to enjoy more autonomy in choosing their partners, and dating became a way to explore relationships and compatibility. The concept of 'going steady' evolved into dating multiple people before committing to a more serious relationship.

The latter part of the 20th century saw a further relaxation of dating norms, influenced by the sexual revolution, feminism, and advancements in technology. The advent of the internet and dating apps in the twenty-first century gave people unprecedented access to a wide pool of potential partners. The traditional gender roles and expectations around dating began to erode, allowing for more fluid and egalitarian interactions.

In today's dating scene, the once-rigid scripts of courtship have become more dynamic and inclusive. And there are both positives and negatives here—even though we tend to only focus on the negatives (it's only human). The emphasis on individual agency, personal choice and open communication has redefined the parameters of romantic relationships. Casual dating, non-traditional partnerships, and a greater acceptance of diverse sexual orientations are now integral aspects of contemporary dating.

Online dating platforms, social media and instant communication have accelerated the pace of forming connections, providing both opportunities and challenges. The ability to connect with potential partners globally has expanded the scope of romantic possibilities, but it has also introduced new dilemmas like ghosting.

And as my participants put it: *ghosting has become a social norm, and kindness is out.*

Standard disturbing behaviour online

My participants tended to normalise bad online dating behaviour, calling it 'standard disturbing behaviour', and often laughing about it, seemingly as a sort of coping mechanism. This behaviour ranged from ghosting, to random requests for nudes, to sending of the ubiquitous unsolicited dick pics, to rude or aggressive comments.

One of my participants, in her early twenties, said the majority of men she met on apps would request nudes, and would sometimes send her unsolicited dick pics after the chat had been shifted onto another platform like WhatsApp or Snapchat. As per Aditi's example of receiving dick pics while on the bus, the burden of labour, the onus to take action against perpetrators, was often on women.

Courteousness versus kindness

Courteousness and kindness, while often linked, are distinct qualities. Courteousness refers to the polite and considerate behaviour we exhibit in social situations. It involves adhering to social norms, displaying good manners, and showing respect for others. Kindness, on the other hand, is more closely connected to compassion. It is rooted in empathy, understanding, and a sincere intention to contribute to the well-being of others.

While courteousness is a valuable social lubricant, kindness has the power to create profound, meaningful connections. The qualities complement each other, and a balance of both can lead to a more compassionate and considerate society.

The importance of kindness

Both kindness and courteousness appeared to be lacking in the modern dating environment—and when I asked my participants to write down the ten things they seek in a partner, kindness was at the top of every list.

People seek kindness in their partners because it is fundamental to human connection. Nobody wants to date a mean person. The idea of 'Treat 'em mean, keep 'em keen' belongs in the eighties, along with shoulder pads and thick blue eyeshadow.

People want to be with someone who's kind.

Awareness is half the battle. Seek to be more kind in the dating world.

♥ Case study: Mei

Empowerment through hooking up

Mei is in her mid-twenties and a talent agent. She recently moved from Melbourne to Sydney for work. She's smart, lively, and a self-declared feminist. She lives in Marrickville with a close friend, and she is looking for love. However, she doesn't use dating apps just for love; she uses them to make new friends, and for sex.

'Initially, I thought dating apps were a bit of a joke. I never thought I'd have to use dating apps to actually *meet* someone. I'm quite extroverted, so I meet men in person all the time—at work, getting a coffee, on the bus . . . wherever. But I got to the point where all the men I met who I was interested in, they weren't interested in me. So then I got onto Bumble and Tinder, more as an experiment. I'd also just moved from Melbourne to Sydney, and I guess it was a good way to meet people and get to know the city.'

'Why did you move?'

'I was offered a new job and it was a good opportunity, but also I think I'd gotten really comfortable with my life in Melbourne, and I sort of wanted to push myself out of my comfort zone. Meet different people, see a different part of the world.'

'And how did it go with the dating apps and Sydney?'

'Well . . . you know, it's busy. There's a lot of chitchat, and a lot of nowhere-going stuff. People aren't there to meet someone. Personally, I used it for a while to see Sydney and find the good places to go to . . .

'I met lots of guys and went on a lot of dates, but none of them really clicked. They were mostly friendships, no chemistry. It's weird how someone can tick all the right boxes on paper but then you meet them, and it's just not there. And then I met a guy on . . . I think it was Hinge. I had started using Hinge because my boss was like, Hinge is where it's at. Anyway, he was this tradie, funny guy. I wouldn't say necessarily my type, but we had this amazing chat online. We shared a lot—which is kind of weird with dating apps, where everything is, 'Hi, how are you?' . . . We had planned to go on a date that weekend, and all week we were talking. Every time my phone pinged I felt like I was a schoolkid, and would blush a bit. Anyway, he took me on an offbeat date where we went to this ritzy auction, and sat down the back and had a laugh about the bids. Like real rom-com sort of stuff. Then we had a fantastic dinner, and I thought . . . geez, I really like this guy. I told myself: Mei, don't sleep with him on the first date, that gets you nowhere—but I did, because we just had this amazing connection. Like crazy chemistry, love match sort of thing. After that, he's planned the next date, and we're texting all week—nothing changes, this amazing connection continues.

'We're planning to go out on Saturday night, but he hasn't given me the specific details yet . . . and then I stop getting messages on Saturday. This is weird because he's a serial texter, always sending messages. Also, I know he's got an Apple iWatch and is always checking it and getting messages . . . so, I know he's seen the messages that I've sent him.

'But I still think there's a reason to it all. It's not until about 8 pm in the evening that I realise I've been ghosted, and I'm there sobbing into a tub of ice cream and watching *A Star Is Born*. My housemate turns up and asked what I was crying about. How bad Lady Gaga's acting is? And I'm like, no, I've been ghosted.

'The worst thing is I was obsessed with this guy for weeks. So sometimes I would think . . . what if he's dead or something, and I'll never know? Eventually, I got to this point where I had to figure it out, and I had his full name, so I looked him up on social media, and discovered that he was alive and well . . . and even worse, one of the jokes I had made on our date, he had used that as a caption to a selfie on Instagram not long after he ghosted me.'

'What do you think happened?'

'I don't know. But this sort of thing happens all the time. After that, I was like . . . I'm done with dating. You know, when I was in my early twenties, I had a really casual attitude towards men. I'd hook up with them, like them, but not get so personally involved, and I wanted to go back to that sort of sentiment. I wanted to get rid of that desperate, I-can't-make-any-relationship-work kind of vibe.'

'And what did you do?'

'Well, I started this intimacy experiment, and it was all about hooking up, being empowered again from a sexuality perspective.'

'Okay, so tell me about how that worked for you.'

'I set up a new profile on Tinder, and basically it was just body shots. You know, really sexual images of bum and boobs, and I had this bio "Here for a good time, not a long time", and basically explicitly said I was looking for no-strings-attached hook-ups. I won't lie, I'm a sexual person; I like a hook-up.'

'And did you keep the other profile . . . the relationship profile?'

'Oh yeah, because I always had my eye on the prize . . . So I thought I'd go back to basics. I started scheduling in guys, like one in the morning, one in the night. Sometimes I'd go through two a day, sometimes none, and in the course of thirty days, I basically had sex with about thirty men, and I got my confidence back.'

'Did you find anything about these men?'

'No it was like name, location—that was it . . . I shared nothing with them. In fact, I remember with the first guy I slept with, after it happened, we were standing on his balcony, and he mentioned something about working in construction, and I thought . . . Wow, I just slept with this guy and I know nothing about him—and that's how I'd like to keep it.'

'Why's that?'

'I don't know . . . Feels like if I know more about them, then I might catch feelings.'

'And did you find that the men respected the parameters that you had set up?'

'Yeah, absolutely. I ended up getting them to come to my house. Because it's just a hook-up, so why should I go out of my way for them? It's not going to progress. There was one guy who looked nothing like his profile, and his breath smelt . . . and I was like, no, I'm sorry, I just can't, and told him to leave. He begged a bit, but eventually he left.'

'You weren't concerned about your personal safety, what with them coming to your house?'

'No. I mean, no. They were harmless. I live with a dude. Not in the slightest.'

'Do you think any of them could have progressed to being more than a hook-up?'

'Absolutely not. I mean, they're there for a hook-up and so are you—nothing more. It's just sex . . . the first guy I hooked up with, I remember we had this really nice chat afterwards, and I did think, he could have been something more if it hadn't started like that. But it did.'

'And why don't you think things can progress if the hook-up kicks things off?'

'I don't know. Because you've agreed to those terms and that's it. Also, once you've been perceived in that sort of light, I don't think you can reverse out of it.'

'Do you mean the kind of girl that someone hooks up with?'

'Yeah, I guess. You go into that category.'

'And did it work out for you? Did you feel empowered?'

'Yeah . . . I guess. I definitely got out of my relationship funk, and eventually I met someone on Hinge. Because I had kept the other profile going . . .'

'And you met someone?'

'Yeah, I did . . . We've been together for a couple of months now, and we've had the conversation, so I've removed my hook-up profile.'

5

Get rid of the shopping list

70 per cent is good enough

You know, I have a lot of women friends, and most of them have this sort of shopping list of the type of man they're looking for. Tall will be somewhere in the mix, nobody wants a short king, and then attractive, of course. Like, we're all supposed to be attractive now! But there's more . . . Some of my friends want men who've already invested in property, or have some particular job, like 'I want a doctor', 'I won't date a tradie' . . . and the list goes on . . . and I think, fuck! That's a lot. I mean, maybe there is someone out there who meets all of those attributes, but you might not actually like them!

The term **short king** is a playful and positive way of refer-
ring to a man who is shorter in stature but still exudes
confidence, charisma and attractiveness. It originated
on social media platforms like X (formerly Twitter) and
TikTok, often in memes and discussions about body

positivity and self-acceptance. The term 'king' traditionally connotes power and authority, and 'short king' reclaims the idea that height shouldn't dictate one's worth or desirability. It celebrates shorter men who embrace their height with pride and confidence, and challenges the way tallness is seen as a desirable, even necessary, trait in men.

This is one of my favourite quotes, and while it is directed towards women (a shortfall), it captures a sentiment which is universal: people have extensive shopping lists when it comes to prospective partners. For a hook-up, not so much, but prospective love matches come with a tick sheet of requirements.

In the realm of modern relationships, the concept of a shopping list of must-haves for partners reflects the focus on the individual, and individual preferences. Dating apps have no doubt enhanced this kind of pickiness. They have led to an increased emphasis on specifying partner preferences, from tangible attributes like physical appearance and lifestyle choices to more abstract qualities like personality traits and values.

Contemporary discussions around partner requirements often revolve around the idea of compatibility. Many people are looking for partners who share similar interests, values and long-term goals. This pragmatic approach to dating is seen as a way to increase the likelihood of a successful and harmonious relationship.

There is also more focus on the importance of emotional intelligence and communication skills in a partner. While physical attraction may be an initial draw, people increasingly recognise the benefits of having a partner who is in touch with their feelings and can express them effectively.

On a train trip I overhead a conversation between three young men. One of them had recently broken up with his long-term girlfriend, or rather, she had broken up with him. The other two men rallied around him in a show of compassion and empathy. The young man in question said his girlfriend had given him three very specific reasons why she had broken up with him. The first: he was argumentative. The second: he wasn't funny enough. And the third: he didn't have a keen interest in social justice or current affairs. My ears pricked up: this seemed to reflect the shopping list approach. Interestingly, this particular man hadn't given up. Instead, he was doing some research to better his communication style, and to increase his understanding of social justice and current affairs. He was even trying to improve his comedic skills.

Financial compatibility is another pragmatic consideration. Individuals often seek partners who share similar financial values and goals. This includes things like spending habits, saving priorities, and attitudes toward financial responsibility.

One woman in her early fifties who appeared on my podcast said she had worked hard to pay off her own home and build up a sizeable nest egg. She was looking for someone who could bring equal financial standing to the relationship, and that was a non-negotiable.

Individuals may also take into consideration how their potential partners engage with technology, their social media presence, and the impact of online interactions on the relationship. Compatibility in the digital realm has become an additional layer in the intricate tapestry of modern relationships. Prospective suitors may now want to size up your social media presence in advance of a meet-up.

Is the shopping list such a bad idea?

Perhaps we're a generation of people who know what we want and won't stand for mediocre love, and lack of compatibility?

I would argue that rigid checklists can limit the potential for genuine connection by focusing too heavily on specific criteria. Intimacy requires flexibility and adaptability, and unexpected qualities or characteristics may contribute significantly to a successful relationship.

Auntie Sima's 70 per cent rule

Indian Matchmaker on Netflix is a reality series that delves into the intricate world of arranged marriages in India. Sima Taparia, often referred to as 'Auntie', is one of the traditional matchmakers featured on the show. The series explores the dynamics of arranged marriages in contemporary society, where individuals are grappling with the delicate balance between familial expectations and personal aspirations.

Auntie Sima uses a mix of experience and intuition to match individuals based on criteria like family values, background and astrological compatibility. She is often given a shopping list of requirements for potential matches, and can rarely deliver on all of them. However, she often advises that *70 per cent is good enough.* By this she means that if 70 per cent of the requirements are there, the rest can be adjusted—there is room for compromise.

Why you should apply the 70 per cent rule

My mother-in-law once told me that she met her husband a couple of times before they were engaged. He was from the same village in Italy (although they now found themselves in Australia). He came to her house and expressed interest in dating her, for the purpose of marriage. She thought him attractive, and kind enough, and discerned that their values aligned. They married, and have been together for forty years, with four children.

I'm not advocating arranged marriages, or swift unions, but there is something to be said for a 70 per cent rule.

The notion that someone will never meet all the criteria one is looking for is an acknowledgment of the inherent complexity of human connections. The reality is that individuals are multifaceted, shaped by unique experiences, backgrounds and perspectives. Expecting someone to perfectly align with every criterion on a checklist ignores the multiplicity of human nature.

We are dynamic entities, constantly evolving and growing. The idea that a single person could encapsulate all the desired qualities, traits and preferences is fundamentally flawed. This realisation is not a dismissal of the importance of compatibility or shared values, but an acceptance that diversity and differences are inherent in the human experience.

Also, individual preferences and priorities can change over time. What may seem like a crucial criterion at one point in life might evolve or shift in significance as circumstances change. This is an argument against establishing a rigid set of criteria for a partner.

Then there's the fact that each partner in a relationship brings their unique strengths and weaknesses. While one person may excel in certain areas, expecting perfection in every facet is unrealistic and sets an impossibly high standard. Relationships thrive on compromise, understanding, and the ability to navigate differences with empathy and open communication.

The idea that someone will never completely meet all criteria can be a liberating perspective. It allows for the appreciation of individual quirks, imperfections and idiosyncrasies that make each person distinct. Embracing the idea that a partner will not fulfil every expectation encourages a more realistic and compassionate approach to relationships, fostering a space for genuine connection rather than a checklist-driven evaluation.

Perfection is an unattainable ideal. Embracing inherent imperfections and recognising the value of compromise and understanding contributes to the resilience and authenticity of connections. The richness of a relationship often stems from the ability to appreciate the entirety of an individual, flaws and all, and to navigate the journey of life together with love, understanding and flexibility.

Too much choice?

The 'paradox of choice' is the idea that having a multitude of options can lead to increased anxiety, indecision and dissatisfaction. This phenomenon is well-documented in psychology and has been explored by various researchers.

Barry Schwartz, a psychologist who wrote about it in his book *The Paradox of Choice: Why More Is Less*, argues that while having options is generally seen as a positive thing, too many choices can overwhelm people, leading to decision paralysis and a decreased sense of satisfaction with the choices they make.

In the context of dating, the paradox of choice becomes particularly pronounced in online dating apps and platforms. With so many potential partners at our fingertips, we may find ourselves endlessly swiping through profiles without ever feeling truly satisfied with any particular match. This abundance of choice can lead to a constant fear of missing out (FOMO), as we worry that there might be someone better suited for us just a swipe away.

Having numerous options can also mean people start thinking of relationships as disposable, and are then more inclined to discard potential partners at the first sign of imperfection or difficulty, rather than investing time and effort into building a meaningful connection.

When it comes to dating, the paradox of choice can lead to increased stress, indecision and dissatisfaction, rather than enhancing the dating experience. It underscores the importance of finding a balance between having choices and being overwhelmed by them, as well as recognising the value of commitment and investment in relationships.

6

Accept yourself as perfectly flawed

Nobody is the main meal

I look at myself and think, there's got to be something wrong here. I have four siblings and they all met people face to face, in the real world, got married, had kids, have jobs . . . bought houses . . . like they've ticked every box. Me? I'm still waiting for things to be kicked off. I'm in my early thirties, I don't like my job, I'm renting—and I can't even convince someone to take me on a date. They either ghost me, or they . . . only contact me if they've got nothing else going on. The 'situationship'. It's like I'm the leftovers. The fact is I'm not the main meal; I'm a quirky side dish, at best. I'm not a perfect person.

This quote is from an incredibly attractive woman with a master's degree and a successful career. Despite her picture perfect social media account, which featured her out and about every weekend at the 'it' restaurant, with the 'it' people, wearing the 'it' clothes, she suffered from bouts of depression and often found herself in bed for long periods of time feeling like a loser—a perfect example of the gap between social media accounts, perceived reality and what's really going on.

The truth in this: none of us are the main meal. We're all exceptionally flawed individuals—some of us certifiably, others just borderline. The sooner we acknowledge the fact we are all imperfect, and that this is okay, the sooner we can move on and lead happier lives, with other equally flawed individuals.

> A **situationship** is a romantic relationship that lacks clear boundaries or commitment. It typically involves two people who are romantically involved but may not define their relationship in traditional terms such as 'dating' or being 'exclusive'. Instead, they might spend time together, share intimate moments and even engage in activities couples typically do, but without explicitly defining the nature of their connection or their intentions for the future.

The dangers of perfectionism

While the desire for excellence can be a motivating force, the relentless drive for perfection in today's society is often detrimental, with its focus on appearance, achievement and constant improvement. Whether it be academically, career-wise, in relationships or looks, the pressure to meet unrealistic standards is relentless.

Social media platforms amplify these expectations, showcasing curated images of seemingly flawless lives and fostering a culture of comparison. They also encourage these ideals through notions like #relationshipgoals. The media plays a part too.

Advertisements, movies and television shows often include idealised versions of beauty, success and happiness.

This constant exposure to unattainable standards creates a distorted perception of reality in the viewer—the belief that perfection is not only achievable but also necessary for a fulfilling life. On the basis of this, people set unrealistic goals for themselves, leading to stress, anxiety and a sense of inadequacy. The fear of falling short of society's expectations, or being perceived as flawed, drives people to either fake it or to push themselves beyond reasonable limits. This idea of 'falling short' was common in my research—the majority of my participants perceived being single as a personal failure, and an indication that there was something fundamentally wrong with them.

The modern emphasis on individualism and self-expression also contributes to this pressure for perfection. In a society that values uniqueness and 'personal brand', people feel compelled to craft an idealised version of themselves. This curated self-image then becomes a source of validation and acceptance—reinforcing the idea that perfection is not only desirable but necessary for social approval.

The obsession with perfection comes at a cost. Mental health issues such as anxiety, depression and burnout are on the rise, as people grapple with the weight of unrealistic expectations. The incessant quest for perfection often leads to a chronic sense of dissatisfaction—people find it challenging to appreciate their achievements when measured against an unattainable standard.

Perfectionism and love

I once worked with an infuriating colleague who seemed to have some sort of narcissistic personality disorder. She talked incessantly about her 'perfect relationship'. It was not unusual for her to use the word 'husband' ten or fifteen times a day. Apparently, in nine years of love they had never once fought.

Yes, never once!

Most people who have been in a long-term (or short-term!) relationship would agree that the odd disagreement, or even row, is to be expected, as two worlds collide—two sets of values, two visions of the future, two individuals! The lack of fighting might mean that one person is subservient, or pretending to be someone else.

Yet the picture this colleague painted of absolute, happy unity made other people in the office anxious. Younger members of staff, who were still negotiating boundaries in their relationships and fought with their partner quite regularly, started to question the validity of their relationships.

In today's society, we're repeatedly told how things should look, by people like my colleague, or via social media, which has a blueprint for every life event, particularly those related to love. This kind of perfectionism can stop people finding love for several reasons, but mainly because it tends to create unrealistic expectations, fear of vulnerability, and a constant need for external validation, all of which can hinder the formation of genuine connections.

Perfectionists often set extremely high standards for themselves and others. This can result in a constant search for an ideal partner who may not exist (the shopping list approach), which can lead to prolonged singledom or a series of short-lived relationships as the perfectionist struggles to settle for anything less than absolute perfection.

Importantly, perfectionism can get in the way of people being authentic. The fear of being judged for imperfections can lead to a guardedness that makes it hard for perfectionists to be themselves. Genuine connection and intimacy require vulnerability and the acceptance of one's flaws, and perfectionism works against both of these. The constant need for external validation and the fear of failure can make dating and forming relationships a very stressful experience for perfectionists. The fear of not being 'perfect' in the eyes of a potential partner can lead to anxiety, inhibiting the natural flow of getting to know someone.

Embracing one's flaws is a crucial step in overcoming the obstacles posed by perfectionism. Recognising and accepting imperfections allows people to be more genuine and vulnerable in their relationships. It creates an environment where authenticity is valued, and both partners can feel comfortable expressing their true selves without fear of judgement.

Embracing flaws also promotes *self-compassion*, an essential quality for building and sustaining healthy relationships. When individuals can extend kindness and understanding to themselves they are more likely to offer the same to their partners, creating a supportive and loving atmosphere.

Embracing our flaws in contemporary culture

Modern films and novels are awash with the notion of embracing your flaws as part of the search for love. *Bridget Jones's Diary* is a good example. In this romantic comedy, Bridget's imperfections and candidness about her struggles with weight, career and relationships make her a relatable character for many. Despite societal pressures and her own insecurities, Bridget learns to embrace her authentic self. In doing so, she not only gains confidence but also attracts the genuine affection of Mark Darcy (Colin Firth). This film serves as a poignant example of how embracing one's flaws can lead to meaningful connections. When individuals learn to accept and appreciate themselves, flaws and all, it paves the way for relationships built on authenticity and mutual understanding.

In the romantic comedy *Crazy, Stupid, Love*, the character of Cal Weaver, played by Steve Carell, also finds his life partner by embracing his flaws and rediscovering his authentic self. Cal's journey begins when his seemingly perfect marriage unravels, and he finds himself navigating the complexities of modern dating. He seeks guidance from Jacob Palmer (Ryan Gosling), a charismatic bachelor with a string of successful romances, but instead of aiming for a polished and idealised version of himself, Cal abandons the notion of perfection and learns to appreciate his genuine qualities. He meets Kate (Marisa Tomei), who is drawn to his authenticity and the sincerity with which he embraces his imperfections, and their connection grows organically.

But why, in the face of popular examples like these, do we shy away from embracing and revealing our authentic selves?

Why can't we accept our messy selves?

One primary reason is the pervasive fear of judgement. Wanting to be accepted, and fearing criticism or rejection, we may choose to present a curated version of ourselves, one that is closer to social norms.

Pressure to meet perceived standards of success and attractiveness also plays a part. Certain types of appearance, qualities and achievements are idealised in our society, and we may feel compelled to mould ourselves to fit them, which may also involve suppressing aspects of our true selves.

Embrace those quirks and flaws!

It's our quirks and flaws that set us apart, make us unique. Learning to embrace these imperfections imbues a person with a certain confidence which can be irresistible.

I'll leave you with this final quote from one of my participants:

I met him at a bar, and he was short and bald, and a little drunk. We'd met on Tinder, and then he'd planned this date. He'd warned me that he was short—but I was just not expecting him to be quite that short, and he was also significantly fatter than I'd expected. Instantly I thought, fuck, no! And I started thinking about how I could get away from him and out of the date. But then he was quite endearing, and funny and silly, and in a very *short* while I quite liked him. In fact, we ended up sleeping together on the first date! And then we became inseparable . . . We've been together for four years and have a child.

7

Invest in yourself

And I mean more than financially

Some of these people I talk to online . . . I just wonder, who are they? They list out the standard interests . . . something about being social, or nature, or beer . . . and that's the end of it. I think to myself, does this person have any substance? What do they actually do? And what will they do if I'm in a relationship with them? Then half the time, or the majority, actually, they'll suggest a date, and it will be loose, like, let's catch up on Saturday. No details. I think: here is further evidence that you have no substance, no kind of creative energy to actually come up with an idea around a date . . . and I lose hope and think, nup, I'm out. This is not the person for me.

The participant quoted here was trying to get a sense of a person online via their likes, dislikes and interests, and finding very little evidence that they had any. They were hoping for some kind of creativity, an impetus to organise, perhaps some suggestions about the form a date could take—and again, nothing. The moral of the story here is: having a thought in your head is sexy.

This was a sentiment echoed by the majority of participants. They were looking for a partner, or a romantic encounter, where the other person had interests, values, and some sort of conviction. They were not after a flake. Participants didn't necessarily think that the other person's interests had to align with their own, but having interests seemed to speak to the character of a person. Their willingness to learn, to change, to be engaged with life were perceived as attractive qualities.

Having no interests also signalled to people that this person was, quite simply, a bore. That they would never want to do anything; that they'd have no enthusiasm about life. There was a sense that such a person would lie about and watch Netflix and order Uber Eats, and while this might be fine some of the time, most people wanted more. It was a major beige flag.

Why the focus on interests and pursuits?

Having interests and pursuits can make someone more appealing to potential partners for several straightforward reasons.

First, having hobbies or interests demonstrates that a person has a life beyond just seeking a romantic relationship. It suggests that they are independent, self-sufficient individuals with passions and activities that bring them joy and fulfilment. This independence is attractive because it implies that the person is not going to be solely reliant on their partner for their happiness or sense of purpose.

Second, sharing interests can be a bonding opportunity. When two people have common hobbies or pursuits, they can connect and spend quality time together doing activities they both enjoy. Whether it's hiking, cooking, painting or playing a sport, engaging in shared interests can strengthen the emotional connection between partners.

Having interests and passions can also make a person seem more interesting and dynamic. People who are enthusiastic about their hobbies tend to be more engaging and lively in conversation. They have stories to share, experiences to recount and insights to offer, which can make interactions more enjoyable and fulfilling.

Pursuing interests often involves personal growth and development, whether it's learning a new skill, exploring a new hobby or challenging oneself to achieve a goal, and this can also be attractive to others.

Avoiding codependency and preserving independence

If you're 'codependent', it means you rely excessively on a partner for emotional validation, support or decision-making. You prioritise their needs, or what you perceive as the needs of the relationship, over your own needs, desires and aspirations. This can lead to feelings of suffocation and resentment.

Maintaining a healthy balance between togetherness and separateness is crucial for the longevity and well-being of a relationship. Ideally, both partners have space to pursue their interests, maintain friendships, and nurture other aspects of their lives outside of the relationship.

Finding solace in our interests

Maintaining—or finding—your own interests is a good way to avoid getting fixated on your romantic life, and also a good mode of self-care.

When I was in my early twenties, I fell for a man I was working with and we were together for a couple of years . . . I was an overly romantic girl, and I'd been waiting to meet the one for a while, and I thought this was it. In India, you don't really date around—or at least not at that time. Maybe things have changed. So there was a pressure there from my family, and even from myself, that this was the one . . .

I threw myself into the relationship, and really just cultivated the person he would want as a wife, from the way I dressed through to the way I cooked. I lost myself in being this person, that lived really to be his partner. It's quite bizarre—because you see me now, very independent. I have a masters in engineering, you know? But I became this person . . . that lived for him.

When he broke up with me I was devastated. I spent weeks in bed, sobbing. I lost five kilos! I thought I'd never be able to face the world—and myself. What was life without him?

And then . . . I had to find myself. A friend of mine recommended taking up a hobby. I thought, who has a hobby? Who *wants* a hobby? But I had no other options. To distract myself from the abyss that had become my life, I started singing again. As a child I had sung . . . and I had a pretty good voice. So I decided to join a choir . . . and surprisingly, it made me feel better. It became something that I liked doing—a distraction from the break-up.

Then it occurred to me . . . this hobby thing has something to it. And I started other hobbies. I started walking in nature, I took up an instrument, and I found myself excited about life again . . . Later, when I thought I'm ready to meet someone new, I found myself with such a full life, and I thought, I want someone who also has a full life, so we can both be independent, but also we can experience the world together . . . And then I found my husband, and I thought, wow . . . he's interesting. He does interesting stuff. I like this man! I like this for me.

As it turns out, hobbies and diverse interests can be a distraction from life's slings and arrows—particularly of the romantic variety. Not only can they make you a more robust, interesting and attractive person, but they can also be a potent source of distraction and nourishing to boot.

A note on creativity

> Every person I meet online is so bland and lacklustre. They never say anything interesting—it's always the humdrum stuff . . . And they can never plan a date. It's always like, oh, let's just catch up. I don't want to catch up—I want something creative, something fun . . . just something. Is it so hard to come up with something?

Curiously, this was a common gripe among participants: a lack of creativity. Ironically, participants would also say that they found themselves being boring—that mediocre behaviours encouraged other mediocre behaviours.

Creativity can infuse interactions with novelty and excitement and foster deeper emotional connections. In relationships, routine and predictability can sometimes lead to stagnation or boredom. Introducing creativity can invigorate the relationship and keep the spark alive. Creative gestures such as planning unique dates, crafting personalised gifts or writing heartfelt letters can demonstrate thoughtfulness and effort, increasing appreciation and affection between partners.

Creativity allows individuals to express their feelings and desires in new ways. Whether it's through art, music, poetry, or other forms of expression, creativity can facilitate deeper intimacy and understanding within a relationship. Couples who engage in creative activities together can also bond over shared experiences, creating lasting memories and strengthening their emotional connection.

Creativity also encourages spontaneity and adaptability—essential qualities in navigating the complexities of romantic relationships. It helps people approach challenges with an open mind, and to find imaginative solutions to conflicts or disagreements. It encourages playfulness and adventure, allowing partners to explore new experiences and grow together.

By infusing relationships with creativity, individuals can deepen their connection, foster intimacy, and keep the flame of romance burning brightly. Whether through grand gestures or small, thoughtful acts, creativity adds richness and depth to the fabric of love, making the journey of partnership all the more fulfilling and rewarding.

Moreover, creativity makes for better lovers.

Become your own Renaissance person

Think about investing in yourself and becoming a Renaissance person, equipped in all sorts of areas of life, from education through to art. Enrich yourself. In doing so, you will become not only someone who is potentially more creative, and more attractive to a possible match, but someone who can also stand resiliently on their own.

A note on safety on the apps

An important way to invest in yourself is to do what you can to keep yourself safe while dating on the apps.

In 2020, my study showed that toxicity and abuse on dating apps was widespread, particularly with regard to women and vulnerable men. This phenomenon is well-documented worldwide.

In January 2023, a national roundtable on online dating safety was hosted by Michelle Rowland, the Communications Minister, and Amanda Rishworth, the Social Services Minister. It included representatives from the online dating sector, various state and territory governments, the domestic violence sector, and advocates for victims. The Albanese government then issued a warning to dating apps: either self-regulate or face mandatory regulation. The industry was asked to develop a voluntary code, and this was finalised in June 2024.

The code encourages apps to verify profiles, provide in-app abuse reporting, and include features for blocking or muting users, to reduce fake profiles and ensure there are prompt responses to bad behaviour. It promotes the education of users on safe dating practices, including recognising and reporting suspicious activity and understanding risks.

Importantly, the code encourages dating apps to collaborate with law enforcement regarding serious misconduct or criminal issues, including sharing relevant data and supporting investigations. (My own research had showed that reports of abusive or unsafe behaviour often went unaddressed.) Accounts that violate safety guidelines are to be terminated across all platforms owned by the company.

Dating apps are also expected to adopt robust data protection practices, such as encryption and secure storage, and to perform regular safety audits.

While this code marks progress, the fact that it is voluntary and not enforceable means some platforms might adopt thorough practices while others make minimal changes. To genuinely protect users, a blend of industry self-regulation and potential legislative measures may be required.

The specific issue of misogyny on dating apps reflects broader societal problems. The influence of people who promote harmful ideologies, like Andrew Tate, exacerbates these issues. A broader approach, focusing on promoting respectful behaviour and establishing clear consequences, is needed.

In the meantime: pay attention to what your potential date says, and how they behave, and if you get the sense you're better off not pursuing a connection—don't. You don't owe anyone on the apps your time, but you do owe it to yourself to date as safely as you can.

♥ Case study: Leo

Racism on the apps

Leo is a thirty-year-old, Chinese-Malaysian-Australian man living in Sydney. He was born in Campbelltown but moved to Sydney in his early twenties after he completed a communications degree. He lives in Darlinghurst, Sydney's gay capital, and is an openly queer man. He has a successful role in one of the largest tech companies in Silicon Valley as the communications director for Asia–Pacific.

Leo is looking for love, intimacy and hook-ups. He uses Grindr, Tinder and Hinge.

'So, you use a couple of different apps. Is your profile the same across all of them?'

'Yeah, absolutely the same. To be honest, I sometimes wonder why I use the three of them because it's kind of the same people across all three apps. But I do think Hinge is a little bit more forgiving—it's more about people wanting to make a genuine connection. But Grindr, in particular, tends to be a lot more cutthroat.'

'What do you mean by cutthroat?'

'Well, it's very much about your appearance. It's all white

dudes with their abs out, in underpants . . . It's very . . . vapid, which is a little bit like what Sydney gay culture is like.'

'Tell me about Sydney gay culture.'

'It's a very small pool of people. Most of us know each other. It is cliquey and very appearance-orientated. There's a certain type of gay man that has more romantic success.'

'And what would that type of man be like?'

'The Aussie bloke type. Kind of like the gay Chris Hemsworth. There's a certain idea of what's masc—masculine, I mean—in the gay space, and yeah, a masc guy is preferred.'

'And what's a masc guy?'

'He's usually white, very muscular, deep voice . . . Almost an updated version of the stereotypical Aussie bloke, but one that fucks men.'

'A deep voice as well?'

'Oh, yeah, 100 per cent. I have quite a gay voice; it's a little high-pitched, and I laugh a lot, and am fairly flamboyant, and that's not on trend in the gay community . . . it's seen as too feminine. So sometimes I'll try to hide my voice. I'll make it sound lower on a first date so that I seem more masculine . . . that sort of thing.'

'Does that make you feel uncomfortable?'

'Of course, there's nothing comfortable about it. I feel like a fraud. But, you know, I'm Asian, so there's no getting around that "feminine" idea.'

'So an Asian man is considered more feminine?'

'Yeah, absolutely. I don't have body hair, and I'm leaner. I guess there's just this idea that Asian men are more subservient. That we're bottoms . . . in everything.' He laughs.

'Would you say Asian men are undesirable in the community?'

'Yes! So undesirable. This is one of the reasons why I don't like using dating apps—I can't deal with the full-on racism. In person, people are a little more tactful, but online, that's all gone.'

'So what type of stuff goes on?'

'It's very common for men to have on their profile "No Asians, just a preference". Very common. And when I see that sort of stuff it really . . . kills me. When I moved to Sydney I thought I'd be living my own personal *Sex and the City*. Instead, I was introduced to this wild environment where nobody wanted to date Asians. I'm from Western Sydney, from an Asian community, so this kind of white world was so foreign to me. It's one of the reasons I go off Grindr or Tinder. It's definitely not a thing on Hinge. But it's certainly still a vibe. I probably get one match a week, or less, so even if people aren't directly saying it, they're thinking it . . . Asians are either ostracised or fetishised. You know how these white men go to these crazy rice queen festivals in Asia, where it's 200 Asian men to one seedy white guy? They're like vultures. It's actually really disturbing, and yeah, it gets me down.'

'So you go off the apps as a result?'

'All the time. I'll spend a couple of months on there, and then the behaviour is too much for me to handle, and I go off them, swear off them, and then a couple of months later I'm back on. In a place like Sydney, you can still meet someone in person. The prejudices are still there if you meet someone in person, but you know, I'm a funny guy, I'm fairly charismatic, so I think I can get around it. But online it's like hitting a brick wall. Then sometimes there's a lull and I get desperate and think, everyone's online, I need to go back on . . . and the merry-go-round starts again.'

'Do you ever feel like you have to change your persona to fit the Aussie bloke stereotype?'

'Yes. But you know at the end of the day I'm still Asian. I can't change that . . . That's the reality of it. I can't discard my ethnicity. But I do things like upload pictures where I look more muscular, where I'm wearing less flamboyant shirts. Where I'm having beers with mates . . . because beers are a very bloke thing. I do try to somehow squeeze into that persona, even though I'm quite aware it's never going to happen.'

'And have you had any luck on the dating apps? Have you met anyone significant?'

'No. I've met hook-ups, and I'm up for a hook-up. I'm happy with a hook-up. But sometimes people want something more. I wonder if I'm going to meet someone myself and have an actual relationship—and these days it seems less and less likely. But then I get to thinking, is this a heterosexual ideal? Do I want this—or is it just a heterosexual ideal of what I should want? The relationship . . .'

'And are you on the dating apps now?'

'I'm on and off. I'll go on . . . and then be so depressed by the quality, the behaviour and all the rest, and then I'll go off and be depressed again! I'm really never going to meet someone if I'm off, so I go back on.'

8

Get beyond the chitchat

Become a conversationalist

I hate the chitchat that goes on, on dating apps . . . I don't use dating apps during the day, while I'm at work, so in the evening I have to catch up with all these chats. Sometimes I'll have multiple chats going at the same time—and I feel . . . well, I feel stressed about having to respond to all these people, but also the stress of having to come up with something new to say. As a guy, I think I'm supposed to provide some sort of direction with starting chats or keeping them going . . . and I have nothing. I have nowhere to go as well. Zilch. I'm a terrible conversationalist. This, I think, is why I can't convert a date.

The lost art of conversation

During the eighteenth and nineteenth centuries, the art of conversation was not only highly valued but considered an essential skill, especially among the upper classes and intellectual elites. Conversation was seen as a form of entertainment, education and social currency.

In aristocratic salons and literary gatherings back then, individuals would engage in spirited discussions on a wide range of topics, including philosophy, politics, literature and the arts. Wit, eloquence and a mastery of rhetoric were highly prized, and individuals competed to demonstrate their intelligence and sophistication via their conversational skills.

Conversation also played a crucial role in romantic relationships. Flirtatious exchanges and wit were often a means of courtship, allowing individuals to express their affection and demonstrate their social prowess.

These days—not so much.

The love letter

These conversations also took literary form. Many famous historical figures have used letters to woo and win over the hearts of their beloveds. Consider the legendary correspondence between poets Elizabeth Barrett Browning and Robert Browning. Their love letters—of which there were 574, running to hundreds of pages—are celebrated for their lyrical beauty and profound emotional depth. Elizabeth's 'Sonnets from the Portuguese' (one of which begins 'How do I love thee? Let me count the ways') were written for Robert during their courtship, and are among the most cherished love poems in the English language.

Today, we might consider ourselves fortunate to receive a love text—and likely it would be littered with emojis, and possibly include a request for a nude!

So what happened?

In the modern world, the art of conversation has undergone a transformation. The advent of technology, particularly social media and instant messaging, has changed how people communicate. Conversations that were once face-to-face are now often conducted via screens, without the nuances of tone, facial expressions and body language.

Modern communication tends to be brief and superficial. Platforms like X (formerly Twitter), with its character limit, encourage succinctness over depth. Texting and messaging apps often prioritise speed and efficiency, sacrificing the richness of language and meaningful exchanges. This can hinder the development of genuine connections and understanding between individuals. Without the opportunity for extended dialogue, conversations may remain shallow, lacking the depth necessary for meaningful interaction.

The rise of digital communication has led to a reliance on emojis, acronyms and shorthand expressions to convey emotions and intentions. While these can enhance clarity in some cases, they often fall short in capturing the complexity of human emotions. Emoticons, for example, may provide a superficial indication of mood but cannot replace the subtlety of facial expressions or vocal intonation. As a result, misunderstandings and misinterpretations are common, contributing to the erosion of meaningful conversation.

Then there's the fact that while platforms like Facebook, Instagram and TikTok offer opportunities for self-expression and connection, they also encourage people to present idealised versions of themselves, carefully selecting which aspects of their lives to share with the world. This can lead to inauthentic interactions, where people are essentially performing rather than interacting honestly.

The constant stimulation provided by social media and digital devices has shortened attention spans and reduced patience for sustained conversation. In a culture accustomed to instant gratification, people are less willing to listen patiently. Many are preoccupied with crafting their next response or waiting for their turn to speak. This lack of attentive listening can hinder empathy and understanding, leading to a disconnect between individuals.

Despite these challenges, it is important to recognise that the art of conversation is not entirely lost in the modern world. Digital communication has also opened up new possibilities for connection and dialogue. Video calls, for example, allow people to engage in face-to-face conversations regardless of geographical distance, bridging gaps and fostering intimacy. Online forums and communities allow people with shared interests to exchange ideas and have meaningful discussions.

When it comes down to it, the art of conversation in the modern world requires a conscious effort to cultivate depth, authenticity and empathy. It involves actively listening to others, expressing oneself honestly and openly, and being mindful of the nuances of language and emotion. While technology has changed the way we communicate, the fundamental principles of meaningful conversation are timeless. By embracing these principles and adapting to the challenges of the digital age, we can preserve and enrich the art of conversation.

Everyone wants 'a good conversationalist with a sense of humour'

Overall, the majority of participants were seeking a match who was a good conversationalist with a sense of humour. Why?

Ultimately, for entertainment—but there's more. Humour

can be a powerful tool for breaking the ice and easing tension, creating a relaxed and enjoyable atmosphere. A person who can inject wit and levity into conversations can put others at ease and foster connection and camaraderie.

Humour adds depth and spontaneity to conversations, making them more engaging and memorable. A good conversationalist with a quick wit can keep discussions lively and entertaining. The ability to find humour in everyday situations can also be evidence of a positive outlook and resilience—qualities that are often attractive to others.

Humour can also be part of emotional intelligence, allowing individuals to navigate sensitive topics with grace and tact. A skilled conversationalist knows when to use humour to defuse tension or lighten the mood without detracting from the significance of a discussion.

Ultimately, a good conversationalist with a sense of humour has the ability to lift spirits, foster connection and make interactions more enjoyable and meaningful.

But not all of us can be funny, and not all of us are naturally good conversationalists. So where to from here?

Learn to converse, and experiment with humour

Becoming a good conversationalist begins with a conscious effort to engage authentically and actively with others. Honing conversational skills involves listening attentively, showing genuine interest in others' perspectives, and responding thoughtfully. Cultivating wit and humour means embracing spontaneity and creativity. You can look for humour in everyday situations, or experiment with wordplay and puns.

Seeking out opportunities to engage, whether through joining clubs, attending events or simply striking up conversations with strangers, can provide valuable practice. Stepping outside of one's comfort zone and embracing the unpredictability of human interactions is essential in cultivating the art of conversation and using humour to connect. And don't be too concerned if you find being funny just isn't your thing. Making an effort to listen well and connect authentically and being open to seeing the funny side will all make a difference.

Ultimately, practising these skills is an ongoing process that requires patience, self-awareness and a willingness to learn from both success and failure. Give it a go! Be prepared to put yourself out there—and perhaps even to be humiliated. Trial and error is required in learning any new skill. Being a strong conversationalist requires a certain vulnerability and authenticity; a willingness to be honest, and even embarrassed. To go out in the world with an open heart and try.

'High-maintenance' women

Most people are familiar with the term 'high-maintenance' when applied to women. It implies that the woman in question is too much hard work; that an easier, more relatable mate would be preferred. In my research, the term was heavily used by heterosexual men.

Sometimes 'high-maintenance' meant a woman was too focused on their personal appearance, or an 'Instagram lifestyle'. However, it was a slippery category. Straight men often said they were looking for a partner who was funny, and a good conversationalist, but 'high-maintenance' could also mean a woman who (according to the man) talked too much, was too smart, too funny (rather than simply being an audience for the man's jokes), or who took the lead in discussions.

Ultimately, it described a woman who was too much to

handle, based on the stereotype that women should be quiet, subservient, opinionless, and always amenable. That they shouldn't be 'difficult', they should smile and be nice, and not take up too much space.

I would argue that making yourself smaller to find a partner (female, male or non-binary) is a recipe for disaster. There's only so long you can repress yourself—your personality, likes and dislikes, desires and interests.

Repressing your personality for a partner can lead to you feeling stifled and unfulfilled. And when you suppress your true self to meet someone else's expectations, you risk losing sight of your own needs, desires and individuality. This can only create resentment. If your partner never truly gets to know the real you, it will be impossible to maintain a genuine connection.

This pressure to be small is not new for women. But if you want a fulfilling relationship, it's worth turning up as your actual self. And remember, if a man can't handle it, there was never the potential there for something real.

9

. . . a delicate balance

Chemistry and compatibility

> I meet people online a fair bit, and I go on dates, and one of the
> things that surprise me is how someone can tick all the right boxes
> in an online environment but then you meet them and there's just
> no spark. A relationship needs a spark. Otherwise it's just a friend-
> ship . . . Actually, you need a spark even for friendships!

The 'sparks' in romantic relationship represent the initial attraction and chemistry between two individuals. Throughout
history, the notion of sparks has been romanticised and
idealised, often associated with intense emotions, passion and
infatuation. But why do we place such significance on sparks in
romantic relationships?

Sparks throughout history

The fascination with 'sparks' in love can be traced back to
ancient mythology and literature, where tales of star-crossed

lovers and passionate romances abound. In Greek mythology, for example, Eros (the god of love) shoots an arrow that pierces the heart of Psyche (a mortal princess), causing her to fall deeply in love with him at first sight. This imagery of love as a sudden, irresistible force has shaped our understanding of romantic attraction.

During the Middle Ages, the concept of courtly love further romanticised the idea of sparks in romantic relationships. The troubadours celebrated the experience of falling in love at first sight, describing it as a divine revelation that sparked the flame of desire in the hearts of lovers.

The Renaissance period saw the emergence of romantic love as an essential component of marriage and courtship. Shakespeare's sonnets, in particular, capture the intensity of romantic longing and desire, portraying love as a tumultuous journey fuelled by sparks of passion and ardour.

In the Romantic period, poets and writers celebrated the experience of falling in love as a transcendent and transformative experience, marked by intense emotional highs and lows. The Romantics believed in the power of sparks to unite souls and ignite the flame of romantic passion, often portraying love as a divine or mystical force that defied rational explanation.

In the modern era, the emphasis on sparks in romantic relationships has persisted, albeit with some changes in perspective. In the twentieth century, with the rise of psychology and sociology, the concept of sparks was analysed through the lens of biology, psychology and social dynamics, shedding light on the physiological and psychological factors that underlie romantic attraction.

Today, while initial attraction and chemistry are seen as playing a significant role in the early stages of a romantic connection, we now recognise the importance of compatibility, communication and shared values in sustaining long-term relationships. But the idea of sparks in romantic relationships persists, reminding us of the magic and mystery connected with matters of the heart.

We all want a spark

The idea that love is some sort of deep magic, catalysed by a spark, is deeply entrenched in our society. This scenario is often depicted in films and novels, and we can come to believe that we should experience this type of electrifying spark when we meet our person. Here are a few salient examples.

In the romantic comedy *When Harry Met Sally*, sparks fly between the titular characters during a road trip they take together. Their witty banter and playful arguments belie a growing attraction that eventually blossoms into love over the course of their friendship. The film explores how sparks of animosity can transform into sparks of passion as Harry and Sally navigate their relationship.

Similarly, in the epic fantasy series *Game of Thrones* sparks of forbidden desire ignite between Jon Snow and Daenerys Targaryen. Their initial meeting is charged with tension and intrigue, as they are drawn to each other despite their respective backgrounds and conflicting allegiances. As they journey together and face numerous challenges, their shared experiences deepen their connection, leading to a passionate and ultimately tragic romance.

And of course we can't go past *The Notebook* by Nicholas Sparks, in which the sparks of romance between Noah and Allie are kindled during a summer romance in their youth. Despite being from different social backgrounds, their instant chemistry and intense attraction cannot be denied. The sparks of their youthful love continue to smoulder over the years, rekindling into a fiery passion when they reunite later in life.

Sparks of attraction can serve as the foundation for a compelling romance in novels and movies, and we may think that's how it should be in real life too.

Married at First Sight and sparks

Reality television shows like *Married at First Sight (MAFS)* in Australia often focus on sparks and attraction among the participants. While the primary premise of the show is strangers meeting and marrying each other without prior knowledge or romantic connection, discussions about sparks, chemistry and physical attraction frequently arise during the filming and airing of the show. For many viewers, such television programs serve as education, or even confirmation of pre-existing views on love and intimacy.

Contestants on *MAFS* often express their hopes of feeling sparks or a strong connection with their assigned spouse on first meeting. Throughout the series, they engage in conversations about their initial impressions, physical attraction and emotional compatibility, all of which contribute to the development of their relationships. Sparks, or the lack thereof, can become a significant topic of discussion among the couples and with 'relationship experts' who guide them through their journey on the show. Viewers witness the dynamics between couples as they navigate their marriages, often observing how sparks evolve or fade over time. Discussions about sparks and chemistry are commonly featured in the episodes, providing insight into the participants' experiences and the complexities of forming romantic connections.

In past seasons of *MAFS* in Australia, there have been instances where couples did not experience a spark or strong attraction upon meeting each other for the first time, despite being compatible on paper according to the show's matchmaking process. For instance, a couple might be matched based on shared values and interests, and because their personalities seemed compatible, but on meeting at the altar they may not feel the spark or chemistry typically associated with romantic attraction. This lack of initial chemistry can lead to challenges and struggles in their relationship. Throughout the season, viewers might see the couple grappling with their lack of spark, attempting to cultivate a deeper connection through various activities, conversations and intimacy exercises. Despite their efforts, the absence of a spark may persist, ultimately dashing their hopes of romance.

While some couples on *MAFS* may experience instant chemistry and sparks, others may find themselves trying to build a relationship without this initial spark. These instances highlight the unpredictable nature of romantic compatibility and the complexities of forming connections, even in unconventional circumstances like those depicted on reality TV.

Tinder—literally named for sparks

The Tinder name comes from the idea of a spark or an initial attraction between people. It evokes the image of igniting a fire or a flame, symbolising the beginning of a potential romantic connection. When users swipe right on the Tinder app, indicating their interest in someone's profile, it's like sparking a flame of attraction. Conversely, swiping left indicates a lack of interest, extinguishing the potential spark. 'Swiping' through profiles on Tinder can be seen as mimicking the process of striking a match, with the hope of finding someone who ignites a mutual interest or connection.

But are sparks at all reliable? Are they a realistic idea of what love should be like? And if not, how should love commence?

What are sparks, and how important are they?

According to UK author Alain de Botton, sparks and chemistry are linked to familiarity. The sudden connection one experiences with a stranger is not a cosmic leap, or a connection between soulmates, but a recollection, a nostalgia of sorts, for the past, or a person from the past, whether that be mother, father or another significant person from our childhood. The sense of connection, the kindling, is merely a jolt of the familiar.

As to how important sparks are, the majority of my participants who had been in long-term relationships said that sparks quickly fade, and that compatibility was more relevant in love. There was an overall sense that sparks and lust were deeply intertwined, but both unravelled quickly in the mundanity of regular life, and shared interests and values were perhaps more relevant. That said, the majority conceded that some sort of spark was required to begin a relationship—otherwise it was just a friendship, and a dull one at that!

Participants also said that sparks could grow, and often people they initially categorised as sparkless became more spark-filled as they got to know them. Throwing out a connection because of the lack of a spark was like throwing the baby out with the bathwater.

One participant said:

I was married for fifteen years, and then we split up . . . and I had to hit the world of online dating, which was very hard. It was just completely unfamiliar territory to me. One of the things that struck me as very different was . . . when I was young, in my twenties I mean . . . I would go on one date every six months, sort of thing, because it's not like I met a lot of potential matches . . . But now you have to go on a date every week. Because you meet so many people on apps, and so I feel like I actively have to be working, going on dates, meeting people and figuring out who's right for me. The big difference is . . . if I go on a date a week, and they're just not the right fit, I think . . . there's no spark, they're just not quite right, and I move on to the next person. But when I was twenty-two, I kind of had to make it work, because I might not go on another date for six months! So I'd think, I've got to make this happen—so even if there wasn't an initial spark, I'd keep working at it . . . and eventually it might come together. Now I think there's too much opportunity, too many people out there, and I think that's negative, because you think the grass is always greener, but likely it won't be! You have to go on more than one date to figure out if you like a person or not.

Sparks versus compatibility

Sparks, characterised by intense chemistry, passion and initial attraction, can ignite the flame of romance and infatuation, while compatibility focuses on shared values, interests, goals, and the ability to navigate life's challenges together. Both elements play vital roles in relationships, yet their significance can vary depending on individual preferences, relationship goals and the stage of a partnership.

Initial sparks, akin to the proverbial 'love at first sight', can be exhilarating and intoxicating, drawing individuals together in a whirlwind of emotions and desire. The thrill of discovering mutual attraction and experiencing a magnetic connection can create a sense of euphoria and excitement that fuels the early stages of a romance. Sparks often manifest through physical attraction, shared laughter and a sense of immediacy, compelling partners to explore the connection further.

But while sparks can set the stage for romance, sustaining a long-term relationship requires more than just initial chemistry. This is where compatibility comes in. Compatibility includes emotional, intellectual and lifestyle alignment between partners. Shared values, beliefs and life goals lay the foundation for a strong and enduring partnership, with mutual understanding, respect and support.

In the long run, compatibility often serves as the glue that holds relationships together through various challenges and transitions. Couples who are compatible tend to communicate effectively, resolve conflicts constructively, and find joy in shared experiences and interests. Their ability to navigate life's ups and downs as a team strengthens their bond and cultivates a deep sense of companionship and trust.

While sparks can ignite the flame of romance, they can also fade over time. If there is also compatibility between the partners, the initial rush of passion may give way to a deeper, more enduring love rooted in shared values, emotional intimacy and mutual respect. In contrast, relationships built solely on sparks may struggle to weather the realities of everyday life as the initial infatuation wanes and partners realise they lack the necessary foundation for a lasting connection.

It's essential to note, though, that the significance of sparks versus compatibility can vary from person to person and relationship to relationship. Some people love the excitement and intensity of sparks, continually seeking the thrill of new experiences and romantic conquests. Others place greater emphasis on compatibility, valuing stability, security and shared values in their partnerships.

Ultimately, the ideal relationship strikes a balance between sparks and compatibility, incorporating the excitement of initial attraction with the enduring strength of emotional and intellectual alignment. Couples who nurture both aspects of their connection can create fulfilling and lasting relationships that withstand the test of time, evolving and deepening with each passing year. Whether sparked by passion or rooted in compatibility, love in its truest form is a dynamic and multifaceted journey that enriches the lives of those who embark upon it.

But take heed of my participants' words: one date can't determine whether there's a spark. You need multiple dates to figure out if there's a flame that can be stoked. However, this is by no means a blanket rule! It only applies if there is a sense of potential compatibility (and an absence of red flags). In a consumer-focused world, where everything is dispensable and just one swipe away, remember that love is diverse, and requires cultivation.

10

Positivity

Prepare your mindset for love

I'm from Russia—we're bleak people, deep but bleak. We drink, we think, we make art . . . but we are also dark. But what I've learned is, in love, nobody wants that. Nobody wants someone hanging about being negative all the time. Life is depressing enough as is! People want someone positive . . . something jovial. I don't mean you have to be toxic about it, and bury your feelings and be happy all the time . . . but take a beat, see the positive stuff. It helps.

The benefits of being positive

We can all get down about love—especially when we've been swiping away with no success for a very long time. As Charlotte cried in *Sex and the City*, 'I've been dating since I was fifteen! I'm exhausted! Where *is* he?' The quest for love can indeed be overwhelming and exhausting.

However, positivity plays a crucial role in love, serving as a cornerstone for healthy relationships and promoting emotional well-being for both partners. Without a pinch of positivity, we're all lost.

In the world of TikTok #relationshipadvice, much information is shared on how to 'get a woman' (or man). It's often based on the concept 'Treat 'em mean, keep 'em keen'. Toxic advice on such platforms encourages users to ghost people and not return phone calls or messages as a way of stepping out of the friend zone and into a relationship. Notably, such advice is based on the idea that the other person is poisonous or destructive—a highly negative view of one's prospective match.

Instead, we should be entering the dating and intimacy world with positivity; with the belief that there are other like-minded people on the planet who are seeking a genuine relationship.

The surprise swingers club

A couple of years ago a friend of mine confided that she had met a lovely gentleman on a dating app. She was in her late thirties and looking for a long-term relationship and a genuine connection, and was making this very clear in her bio, and also in her chats with prospective matches. She had met a few men on dating apps, and gone on a few relatively pleasant dates. There hadn't been a connection, but nonetheless, she had met some new people, and tried a few of the hip new restaurants in town.

Then she met someone she was very interested in. Their chats felt like kismet: they had the same sense of humour, interests and view on the world. Then he suggested they meet up for dinner on a Friday night. He planned the evening in detail. She loved this. One of her key gripes about dating apps was men with nebulous plans like, 'Let's catch up at the end of the week'. Here was a man with a plan, and it wasn't just any plan: it was the best restaurant in town, the one with a waitlist a mile long.

She was excited about the date. There were butterflies. She felt like she was on the precipice of a big story . . . maybe a big love. It occurred to her that this could be the man she was looking for.

They met at the restaurant, and all seemed good. He was tall, attractive, funny, exactly as she had expected, and their chat continued to be sublime. After the buffalo mozzarella, cavatelli and a couple of glasses of vino, they started confiding secrets, and he suddenly declared, 'I've always wanted to go to a swingers club.' The statement shook her, but she maintained her calm demeanour. He hadn't seemed the type, especially given they'd both said they were looking for a committed and monogamous relationship. She said, 'Oh, really?' Taking this as a sign of potential interest, or at the very least a nod to continue, he said, 'Actually, there's a swingers club just down the road . . . I've always wanted to try it. Maybe we should after this meal.' She shook her head, saying, 'No. No, absolutely not.' She took another sip of her vino and concluded that this man wasn't after a committed relationship—he was on dating apps to find a date so he could go to the swingers club down the road. The selection of this particular restaurant was not thoughtful, it was just convenient, so he could take her to the swingers club down the road.

She concluded the dinner, blocked him in the cab back home, and proceeded to delete all her dating apps. Two months later, she decided she wasn't meeting anyone in real life, and it was time to cut her losses and return to the apps that had brought her 'swingers club guy' (as he was colloquially now known among our circle of friends). But she could never really eradicate swingers club guy from her thoughts, and she began every interaction with a man with a negative mindset: they were all tarred now with the swingers club brush.

It's easy to be positive when you're winning

It's easy to be positive when things are going your way. If every man or woman you've met has been an America Ferrera or Dev Patel type, and never suggested a swingers club, it's easy to assume such a pattern will continue. There's a biological reason for this: emotional memory. Human brains are not only good at remembering facts but also at recalling the emotions associated with those facts. This emotional memory plays a crucial role in how we perceive and react to the world around us. Positive experiences often leave behind a residue of positive feelings, making it easier to maintain a positive outlook. Negative experiences can leave emotional scars, leading to a more pessimistic view of similar situations in the future. So if you have an experience like swingers club man in the mix, it's only natural to feel like swingers club man two is just around the corner, and waiting for you at a fancy restaurant.

Then there's confirmation bias, which motivates people to interpret and recall information in a way that confirms their preconceptions. If you've had many positive experiences, you're more likely to expect positive outcomes, which makes you notice and remember positive events more readily, reinforcing your positive outlook. The same goes for negative experiences leading to a more negative outlook. It's a spiral. The result, in dating, can be this kind of dating doom, where we start to assume every man or woman is the same, and the negative mindset takes root.

After a series of such interactions, it's hard not to assume that more heartbreak or disappointment might be just around the corner, which gives rise to gendered statements like 'They're all the same!' It can be difficult to see beyond this negative world view. Here's one participant's story:

I was in my forties, and at that point I was quite committed to being alone. I felt like I'd missed the boat—when I was young and attractive, they wanted me and I didn't want them, and now that I wanted them, they didn't want me. I had a sense that I was going to spend the rest of my life living with my parents, and then . . . when they passed, it would just be me, alone.

So when I met this woman out of the blue, and she liked me, and I liked her, it seemed too good to be true. She didn't have any of those traditional red flags that people in my age group tend to have—things like day drinking, for example. She seemed incredibly normal. Compassionate, even. Kind . . . And I kept thinking . . . this just can't be right. Something's going to come out at me from nowhere, and I'll discover she's nuts, or married or something.

I was so sure this was going to happen I kept looking for things, and being . . . aha, see! I told you so! Eventually she said to me, I actually can't deal with your behaviour anymore. I feel like you're constantly trying to catch me out.

I had to face myself, and I had to change my mindset . . . I had to become positive about relationships and her, and sort of set the disappointment aside, and that's hard to do, because you spend a lifetime building up that disappointment, that bitterness. It becomes your armour. It's easier to believe that things will go wrong rather than right.

I had to change, otherwise I would have lost her.

A positive mindset anticipates happiness, joy, health and favourable results. If you adopt this mental attitude, you teach your mind to expect success, growth and favourable outcomes, in love and all other areas of your life.

Why is it so hard to be positive?

Believing that things will go wrong rather than right, especially in relationships, can be attributed to negative bias, where negative experiences are remembered more vividly than positive ones. If we have faced disappointments, betrayals or hurt in our relationships, these negative memories can easily overshadow any positive interactions, leading us to expect similar outcomes in the future. This tendency is reinforced by confirmation bias, where we selectively notice and recall information that confirms our pessimistic views, ignoring evidence to the contrary.

Additionally, expecting the worst can serve as a form of emotional armour, a way to protect oneself from the pain of potential disappointment. This self-protective mechanism makes it feel safer to anticipate failure rather than risk the vulnerability associated with hope. For many, the fear of being hurt again is so daunting that they prefer to adopt a defensive stance, thinking they're softening the potential blow of another letdown. Over time, such expectations can become a part of one's identity, making it difficult to imagine a different scenario without feeling unrealistic or naive.

Changing this entrenched mindset requires conscious effort and sometimes professional guidance to develop a more balanced perspective. It involves challenging these ingrained biases and fears, actively seeking out and remembering positive experiences, and developing resilience so that fear of potential disappointment doesn't prevent one from fully engaging in relationships. This shift is about learning to trust—not just in others, but also in one's own capacity to handle whatever outcomes life may present—and leads to a healthier and more hopeful view of personal connections.

Try a dash of positivity

They're not all the same—it's impossible for them to be so. And you are not hated by the gods, the universe, the powers that be. The idea that the universe is personally against us can feel compelling during tough times, but it involves a couple of logical and psychological leaps that, when examined, reveal it to be unreasonable and a bit egocentric. The universe is vast and impersonal, involving countless processes that don't have a specific agenda for or against anyone. Believing that the universe is against us is egocentric because it places us at the centre of cosmic events, with our particular life as the focus of the universe's attention. In reality, the challenges we face are experienced by many others, and attributing personal misfortune to cosmic forces can be a way of not recognising the commonalities of human experience.

The universe is not blocking you from finding the love of your life. You are not unlucky in love.

What you really need is a lick of positive thinking. The universe doesn't care who you date, and might accidentally, in the chaos of it all, send Prince or Princess Charming in your direction.

But if you're committed to not seeing them for who they are, you might just miss out.

♥ Case study: Sandra

When love surprises you

I was married a couple of months before I travelled to Australia. I knew the man, but not well. He was from the same town as me, and I knew of him. One day he went to my parents' house and said he wanted my hand in marriage. My parents came to me and said . . . he came from a good, hardworking family, and they thought this was a good opportunity for me.

They had three other children, and this was after World War II. There was a lot of poverty. A daughter leaving the house with a reasonable man was a good thing.

The only catch was, he was travelling to Australia. For good. Like a lot of the men in my town. They were going to Australia, or Argentina, or elsewhere. There was no work in Italy. So they were going to make their fortune, or at least a reasonable life.

I didn't want to go to Australia—I was a 17-year-old girl. I didn't speak English. I was afraid. My friends and family were all in town in Italy. I cried that night when they told me. Imagine telling a young girl today she has to go halfway across the world with a man she doesn't know and stay there as his wife.

This is what happened.

Eventually I said I would go, that I would marry him. I knew I was a burden to my family, and I felt pressure from them to go. So I said yes.

We were married at the local council. He was early and I was late. Then directly after that, he left. He already had the ticket on the boat for Australia, and he paid for mine, but I was set to leave two months after him.

I had never been on a train, let alone a boat for a month.

I took my little suitcase, and I went, because I had to. My parents knew a couple of other people who were travelling to Australia on the boat, and introduced me to them so I wouldn't be so alone. One was a man from a village close by.

I was incredibly sick on the boat—seasick. I was in my cabin all the time.

And this man looked after me. We were a similar age, and I remember thinking he was so handsome. He would make jokes, and bring me food, and we would talk about what Australia was like. He was afraid too, like me. His brother was already there, and said there was work and money. But he hated the idea of leaving home. Like me.

Six weeks on a boat is a long time.

I fell in love with this man—we both fell in love. We hatched a plan about how when we arrived at the dock in Australia, we would leave together, and take off. My husband would be waiting there for me and we knew we had to be quick, and smart.

He wasn't really my husband—we had met a couple of times in Italy, that was it.

So that's what we did. We arrived in Australia and started running, and we ran so far, all the way to Melbourne, where his brother was. It was so clandestine, such a rebellion and an adventure. I was a small-town girl who had never left her village. This was craziness.

But we were so far from home, and I loved him.

We were married in Melbourne, and spent forty years together and had three children. He died of cancer ten years ago.

My parents forgave me eventually, even though it brought them a lot of shame.

Of course we had our arguments, our fights. Love is not easy. It's work. Life is work. But you have to keep going.

I never went back to Italy, and I loved him always, maybe because he got me out of that life—the one they had made for me, but I didn't want.

Why is it all about finding love, not keeping it?

We're not taught how to keep love

From ancient myths to modern rom-coms, the pursuit of love has been celebrated, revered and romanticised. Yet the stark reality is that we're often better at finding love than keeping it. The chase for the elusive spark of love is glorified, while the art of nurturing and sustaining it remains underexplored.

Think of Shakespeare's *Romeo and Juliet*, where the intensity of young love collides with the harsh realities of life, culminating in tragedy. Or films like *Titanic*, which showcase the exhilarating highs and heartbreaking lows of romantic love. These stories reflect our fascination with the initial rush of infatuation . . . and lack of interest in what comes after.

Because of this, we often neglect the essential skills needed to maintain love. All too often, relationships falter not because of a lack of love, but because of a lack of understanding and communication. We're not taught how to love; we're left to stumble through our relationships without a guide.

The consequences are evident in divorce statistics around the world. In Australia, for instance, divorce rates have remained consistently high, with nearly half of all marriages ending in separation. While some may attribute this to changing societal norms or economic factors, at its core lies a fundamental misunderstanding of what it means to love and be loved over the long haul.

The notion of 'happily ever after' perpetuated by fairytales and romantic comedies offers little guidance for navigating the complexities of real-world relationships. Contrary to popular belief, love is not a static destination but a dynamic journey filled with twists and turns and sometimes . . . inertia. True happiness in love is not found in grand gestures or sweeping declarations but in the everyday moments of connection, understanding and mutual support.

In a world where relationships are increasingly commodified and disposable, cultivating enduring love requires focus and resilience. It means showing up for each other not just in the honeymoon phase but also during the inevitable rough patches.

Ultimately, the pursuit of love is not just about finding a soulmate but about becoming a better version of ourselves in the process. It is about learning to see beyond the superficial allure of attraction and embracing the messy, imperfect reality of human connection.

So how do you keep the spark alive? Maintain respect and kindness? And not stray . . . given an endless array of other Cinderellas and Prince Charmings out there?

I asked these questions of my willing participants, many of whom had survived the seven year itch, and some of whom had been with their partners for forty years. I asked them how they did it, and what were the ten most important qualities to keeping love in a world obsessed with the disposable.

PART TWO

Ten ways to keep it

1

Love as work

The myth of effortless romance

Number one—love is not easy. It takes work. My partner and I saw a counsellor a couple of years back because we'd hit an impasse. We'd spent seven years together. We'd gotten married, but there was no respect or kindness anymore. We were on the road to disaster. My partner was very open to seeing a counsellor—he'd been to therapy before—whilst I saw it as strange, a little intrusive. It wasn't how I usually dealt with my issues . . .

But it changed things for us. She gave us the kinds of tools we needed to rebuild the relationship, nurture it, cultivate it . . . But you have to keep working at it every week; every day. Don't get me wrong, this is a journey. But I'm proud of the journey—I love my partner. This is the most important relationship of my life and I'm willing to invest in it.

Many of my participants in long-term relationships said they had sought the assistance of a counsellor at some point. Others said they were proud of how they had overcome adversity, and difficult situations. Overall, there was a sense that love and long-term relationships weren't easy, in spite of the common idea that they should be.

Busting the myth of effortless romance

Love has been idealised as a force that effortlessly binds two souls together in blissful harmony. In our contemporary culture, there's a pervasive belief that *love should be easy*; that when you meet the right person, love will flow effortlessly.

From bestselling novels to blockbuster movies, we are inundated with stories of whirlwind romances and fairytale endings, where love conquers all without the slightest hint of struggle or conflict. Finding 'the one' is presented as the ultimate goal, with little attention paid to the hard work required to sustain a fulfilling relationship beyond the initial infatuation. This model of love is seductive because it offers the promise of instant gratification and eternal happiness.

Here's one participant's story:

> When I met Jack it just instantly felt right. There were no games. He would just respond to my texts. We would go on dates. We connected; we understood each other. It wasn't like the usual stuff, where everything felt difficult; where I would just be trying to figure out what was going on with them constantly. It felt easy. A month and half later, we were official and I met his parents. Some people are saying to me that we're moving too fast, but I don't think so—when you know, you know.

This account contains several popular conceptions of love, from 'when you know, you know' through to the idea that love is easy. This participant failed to realise that in the early stages of a relationship we are often putting our best selves forward, but that over months and years our more difficult selves surface, and we can lose the kindness and respect which helped bind the relationship together. The 'easiness' that once characterised the relationship can disappear, and things become hard.

The truth is that long-lasting love is anything but easy. It requires patience, compromise, and a willingness to confront challenges head-on. Love, like any worthwhile endeavour, demands effort to thrive. Yet the idea that love should be easy often leads people to give up at the first sign of struggle, believing that if love is meant to be, it should require no effort at all. Instead of dealing with the inevitable obstacles and conflicts, they may walk away in search of a love that better aligns with their idealised fantasy.

Love is not a passive state but an active choice that requires ongoing effort and investment. This work takes many forms, including effective communication, emotional vulnerability, and a commitment to nurturing the bond between partners.

Another participant says:

> I went through this period of time with an ex of mine where we would have these huge rows about things . . . just conflicts in values, or feeling unloved in little ways, you know . . . We'd fight, and basically declare that it was over, and that would go on for a couple of days and then we'd work things out. I think you become a little addicted to the drama of that sort of thing, because everyday life with a partner can be kind of dull . . . But eventually it became a big problem, and we ended up breaking up because we fought too much.
>
> I do think that relationship had potential. We were just willing to throw in the towel easily. We didn't necessarily want to do the work to understand each other and be more compassionate.

The challenge of the mundane

When we're in love, life is no longer mundane. We're suddenly the protagonists of a romantic story; we're special and unique.

But the thrills of new love can be swallowed up by the mundanity of everyday life. We move in together and suddenly we're faced with the prospect of bills, taking out the rubbish, cleaning, cooking and, lord forbid, *shared bathrooms*! That sense of immortality and magic evaporates, replaced by everyday life, boredom. We want relationships to be solid; we want to live together, get married, create families—but in doing so we remove the excitement and, yes, impermanence associated with the spark and passion of love. *We put a cardigan on love.* Some people love to wear cardigans; others are terrified by them. They end up feeling more like they're in a straitjacket, and compelled to act out.

The mundane aspects of life together can gradually dull the initial spark of a romantic connection. Couples may find themselves *arguing over minor issues as a form of dramatic relief from life's dullness*, and these conflicts can accumulate, as they did for my participant, testing their resolve to stay together.

Neglecting ourselves and what we really want

As relationships mature, the excitement of newness can fade into the background, replaced by predictability and routine. Maintaining individuality is crucial, but partners often get so entangled in their roles—be it as parents, professionals or caretakers—that they neglect their own identities and desires. We can become Mummy or Daddy; the worker bee paying bills. Our dreams and passions sometimes take a back seat to earning a living: the artist becomes a creative designer for a multinational corporation; the writer becomes a copyeditor for a mortgage broker; the athlete becomes a weekend soccer parent. With these changes, we can disappear, lose our passion as an individual, and the sense of mystery and allure that initially drew two people together can evaporate.

This is one participant's story:

We were married for ten years when I cheated. I was on a work trip overseas and travelling with a colleague, and it happened. There had been a flirtation with us for a while, and it was kind of sustaining me, this sort of emotional fling at work. I never intended on taking it to the next level. It was more about just having that sense of excitement, the butterflies, feeling special—all that silly stuff. But then things escalated. It was the worst decision I ever made . . .

I came back and after months of living with the guilt of it, I eventually told my wife. I told her it was a mistake and I wanted to be with her . . . but I don't think she's ever forgiven me. We went to see a counsellor for a long time afterwards, but we really should have seen the counsellor beforehand.

You see, when we met it was so exciting. I'm Lebanese and I guess my parents always saw me marrying from within our culture, and when I met my wife, she was this beautiful blonde free spirit, and I guess so was I when we were young. There was something almost forbidden about the relationship. But at the same time I knew we clicked; there was a mutual understanding between us about the world, about how things should be. I knew she was the one for me.

But ten years in, three sons later, jobs, mortgages and all the rest . . . I just didn't recognise that person in her anymore. She was someone completely different, and so was I. We weren't exciting to each other anymore. It was just the boring day-to-day stuff. She wanted to see a counsellor, but I just thought it was stupid, and I was living my fantasy with this other woman.

Of course, it all came crashing down when I slept with my colleague—and the guilt of it all, I don't think I'll ever forgive myself. I love my wife, I love my family—I just don't think I made space for our relationship.

Sustaining love takes work

In maintaining relationships, research shows the importance of regular communication, empathy and conflict resolution skills. It's also vital to address deeper emotional issues, to increase understanding and connection. Emotional responsiveness and vulnerability are crucial, as these help create a secure bond between partners. However, as demonstrated by my participants, maintaining novelty and autonomy is equally crucial.

Navigating the challenges of love-term love might not necessarily involve professional counselling, but it does require a concerted effort to work things out, recognising that managing the inevitable clashes in a relationship demands dedication.

Put the same effort into love that you do in other areas

I interviewed Melissa Hobley, at the time the global chief marketing officer for OkCupid (and now chief marketing officer of Tinder) about love and intimacy and dating apps. She talked about the popular idea of love and relationships as 'easy'.

I have friends who run marathons, and are the CEOs of companies. They train for marathons on a daily basis: complex exercise routines, eating habits, etc. They do courses for work, and long hours . . . but when it comes to love, they're like, this is just going to happen. Someone's going to walk right up to me and declare they're the love of my life, and we'll be together till the end of time, no work required.

The expectation that love should come easily and without effort stands in stark contrast to the dedication people display in other areas of life, such as their career or physical fitness. This disconnect underscores a vital truth: just as success in a marathon or in the boardroom requires dedication and hard work, so too does building and maintaining a meaningful relationship. It's important to challenge the idea that love should be effortless, and to embrace the idea that real, enduring connections grow from sustained effort and nurturing. Just as we train and prepare for other challenges in life, love too deserves our energy and commitment if we are to expect lasting and fulfilling results.

2

I choose you

Prioritising one person

Most participants in the study recognised that some of their past relationships had the potential to succeed, but various factors got in the way. Common reasons included poor timing, a lack of commitment, and a focus on personal goals over the relationship. Many admitted they lacked the self-awareness at the time to understand their part in the relationship breakdown, often summarising their experience with statements like, 'Could it have worked out? Yeah, probably, but it didn't.'

This ambivalence was common. Many people avoided committing to a relationship, believing that a better option was always just one swipe away. The grass was always potentially greener elsewhere, encouraging a continual search for something newer and better. This devalued current relationships and the unique qualities of partners. It made romantic connections seem disposable. There was rarely a definitive sense of: 'I choose you.'

Why is it hard to choose one person?

These days, autonomy and flexibility are prioritised, which favours fleeting connections that provide immediate satisfaction without long-term commitment. This approach to romance mirrors broader trends towards individualism and self-fulfilment.

Digital technology and social media have only intensified this. On the dating apps, people can quickly connect with partners and just as swiftly discard them, leading to fragmented and superficial interactions, and a sense of insecurity and alienation. The pursuit of temporary connections can offer momentary excitement and validation, but often results in disillusionment, and a cycle of dissatisfaction.

Choice and commitment to one person seem impossible, and we can be haunted by the fear that there is someone better out there. There's also the fear of vulnerability—nobody wants to choose someone only to find that person doesn't choose them back.

Putting our hearts on the line can seem like a recipe for disaster, but if we want to be part of a long-term relationship, it's required. This kind of commitment makes us willing to put in the work to sort out that argument, or that miscommunication, or that bump in the road.

The 'I choose you' is necessary in a lasting relationship.

What the Ancient Greeks knew

The Greek concept of *pragma* refers to a type of love that emphasises practicality, long-term commitment and enduring companionship. Unlike the passionate and spontaneous *eros*, or the playful and affectionate *ludus*, *pragma* is characterised by its rationality and groundedness. It is the love that develops over time, rooted in shared values, compatibility and mutual respect. *Pragma* was seen as the foundation of a stable and harmonious household, where partners worked together towards common goals and supported each other through life's challenges.

In contemporary society, *pragma* continues to be a useful guiding principle in long-term relationships. Couples who prioritise shared values, communication and compromise are more likely to sustain lasting love and companionship. *Pragma* reminds us that love is not solely about passion and romance, but also about commitment, understanding and mutual support.

Where 'I choose you' comes in

Interestingly, many of my participants were married, and yet the majority also said they could see their partnership unravelling. Here was the ambivalence or apathy again. They'd say things like, 'I'd like this to last forever—but I also have to be realistic.' It was almost as though the utopian idea was to be together forever, but reality got in the way.

In this ambivalence or apathy was also a kind of non-commitment, an unwillingness to choose one person, lest it end in disaster. So you get statements along the lines of: 'I think this person is great, but I can't put all my eggs in one basket. We've been together for fifteen years, and I hope this is my forever person, but in life you can never really say.'

> This hedging of bets sounds like a kind of postmodern pragmatism, but at some point you have to choose; you have to put your eggs in one basket and risk the frittata, otherwise you'll always be looking, or hatching an escape plan, rather than being in the moment and enjoying the current relationship or person.

Be willing to be vulnerable

Extensive research has shown that vulnerability helps to create authentic connections, as well as building resilience and increasing empathy. At its heart, vulnerability is not a weakness but a courageous act of living wholeheartedly. It requires showing up and being seen, even in the face of uncertainty, risk and emotional exposure.

This means embracing our imperfections, owning our stories, and allowing ourselves to be truly known by others in a world that often values perfection and invulnerability. Vulnerability paves the way for deeper relationships. And yes, it also means putting our heart on the line.

Vulnerability is pivotal in developing intimacy and trust. It involves creating a safe space where partners can express their deepest fears, insecurities and desires without fear of judgement or rejection, allowing them to genuinely connect with and support each other.

However, it can be daunting to be vulnerable in relationships, especially in cultures like ours, that view it as a sign of weakness or inadequacy. We put up emotional barriers, worried about being rejected, shamed or betrayed. Yet it is through vulnerability that we get to experience real love and connection. We have to show up authentically and risk disappointment if we want to experience that. When we choose and invest in one particular person, vulnerability is essential.

Australian men as 'laid-back'

Australian men are often stereotyped as laid-back rather than passionate lovers. They are depicted as rugged, independent characters with a love for adventure and the outdoors, embodying a carefree spirit rather than the intensity typically associated with great lovers.

Australian culture places a value on looking relaxed and not appearing to try too hard. The ethos of 'mateship' and egalitarianism promotes modesty and the avoidance of overt displays of ambition or emotion. This can extend into romantic relationships, so that men feel they must play the 'cool' Aussie who approaches love with an easy-going attitude. Media and entertainment often reinforce these perceptions by portraying Australian men as rugged and independent, more interested in adventure than emotional depth or intimate relationships.

However, stereotypes do not capture the full spectrum of any group's experiences and identities. Many Australian men diverge from this archetype, bringing passion, intensity and commitment to their relationships. The idea that they always prioritise being cool ignores the realities of successful relationships, which demand effort, commitment and vulnerability.

Like people from any cultural background, Australians men (and women) are fully capable of being profound lovers when they approach relationships with authenticity, vulnerability and a readiness to engage emotionally with their partners.

How not saying what we feel gets in the way

Numerous relationships fizzled out over the course of my research, either right at the beginning or later on, because participants hesitated to be honest about their feelings. For many, it was simply because they were too proud or embarrassed to be honest about how they felt, and this thwarted many potential connections. For instance:

I was really into this guy. I didn't meet him online. He lived upstairs. We had a really nice vibe—he was an actor and he was quirky and fun . . . and one day, I was at his place and something just happened between us, and we slept together. It was light and fun and we had a great time—and then after that, he texted me and asked if I wanted to go for a drink the following week. I said sure . . . and then an hour before the date he cancelled on me. I thought that was pretty rude, and the excuse was a bit lame, so I assumed he wasn't into me. Then he texts me again, and wants to make a new plan, but at that point I'm kind of pissed, and I don't just want to say, yeah, I'm available . . . So I say no . . . And then it just fizzled, and got really awkward—like, we could barely say hello to each other in the hallway. I had to move, I felt so weird about it! It's a shame . . . I really liked him.

This kind of story was common. Many interpreted the other party's actions as a lack of effort, and this was interpreted in turn as disinterest. Conversely, when the other party made an attempt to demonstrate interest, participants frequently felt a compulsive need to preserve a balance by appearing less interested, leading to unresolved tension and friction. A mutual reluctance to embrace vulnerability prevented the open discussion of feelings, and potentially promising connections quickly unravelled.

Prioritising one person

Choosing to commit to one person in love and prioritising them above others is fundamental to nurturing an intimate (monogamous) relationship. This commitment involves not only a conscious decision to be exclusive, but a continuous effort to invest time, energy and emotional resources into the partnership. In a world filled with endless distractions and temptations, prioritising one's partner sends a powerful message of love, loyalty and devotion.

3

Use your words

Communication

I think you can go a year of your life, maybe more, and not really have talked to your partner. You just get sucked up into the daily grind—and that's it. You get home, it's late, you're tired, fed up with colleagues and bosses, and you just want to put the kids to bed, and have a glass of wine and watch Netflix. Sometimes I'm all talked out, you know?

But then it's like this person is a stranger . . . and at some point things just fall apart, and you find yourself wondering, what actually happened?

It may seem inconceivable (ludicrous, even!) that two people sharing a home could spend a year or more without ever talking about their thoughts, fears and hopes, yet this is surprisingly common. Over time, the familiarity of living with someone can make them seem mundane and uninteresting. We can fall into the trap of believing we know everything there is to know about our partner, and as a result, we stop paying attention or really showing up. Instead, we reserve our most vibrant, engaging sides for others—perhaps coworkers or friends.

In the early stages of a relationship, we naturally present our best selves to our partners, but as the novelty fades and we grow accustomed to each other, a less appealing version of ourselves can emerge—one that may lack kindness and empathy. We stop sharing our stories, secrets and desires. This withdrawal can transform us into strangers living under the same roof, and gradually erode the intimacy that once connected us.

In addition, the digital world can be omnipresent. We may find ourselves scrolling on our phone, or watching Netflix, then realising the person sitting on the couch next to us is doing the same thing. In the glow of those digital devices, we may stare at them wondering, who is that person?

My research repeatedly highlighted how important effective communication is in healthy relationships.

Assuming our partner will just know

I often thought my partner would just know when I was upset—especially if I'd been talking about [a topic] for some time. Like, if I'd been complaining about a friend for weeks, you'd think he'd understand it was a development on that front . . . The 'What's wrong?' question frustrates me. How can they not know?

The assumption that our partner should just intuitively know what's going on with us is a common one, but it can lead to misunderstandings, frustration and, ultimately, strain on the relationship. It's as though we think this person is inside our minds, living our experiences with us. In reality, they are a completely separate person and to some degree will always remain a mystery. As will we!

Movies, television shows and novels often show partners effortlessly understanding each other's thoughts and feelings without the need for clear communication. These depictions can create unrealistic expectations and fuel the belief that true love means being able to read each other's minds. But remember: these people are figments of someone's imagination.

Gender roles also play a part in shaping misconceptions about communication between partners. There's an assumption that women are more attuned to emotions and should be able to anticipate their partner's needs, while men are expected to be stoic and self-sufficient. People can end up believing the false and dangerous idea that emotional expression and communication are the responsibility of one partner, rather than a shared responsibility between both parties.

Past experiences can also influence our expectations in relationships. People who grew up with a lot of talk in their households may be used to constant communication, but unaware that certain types of communication are more useful than others. One of my participants said:

> I grew up with two sisters, so I come from a background of: you talk all the time about everything . . . But interestingly, not all of that communication is useful. For example, I'd complain about things, but also I wouldn't say things like: this is what I need from you. I'd still leave some stuff up to the imagination. I needed help in terms of [finding] a more meaningful way of communicating.

If we're not talking to our partner, who are we talking to?

It's very important to retain our friendships and other relationships. We can't get everything from one person—that's the definition of codependency. Leading a full and vibrant life and retaining our individuality and our friendships goes towards a successful and fulfilling relationship. Having diverse sources of emotional support is healthy and helps maintain a balanced perspective that isn't overly dependent on one person.

But things can go too far in the other direction.

> I used to speak to a girlfriend of mine three to four times a day on the phone. Maybe more. When I was driving to work I'd call her, on my lunch break, when I was driving home, and so forth. We'd send a million texts as well. Most of the discussion revolved around how much we hated our partners, our jobs, our lives. It was really cathartic getting this stuff out. I was kind of addicted to it. We were so obsessed with just talking about this stuff, and we were basically resolved [that] we had no way out, we had to stay with our partners essentially until they died, and we had to keep on with our jobs and all the rest. But we had each other.
>
> Then we had a falling out . . . and we stopped speaking, and for about a month I literally felt withdrawals, like I was addicted to purging all this negative stuff and having it reinforced by her . . . And then it started to go away. I started talking to other people, including my partner, and it felt so much more balanced, and so much less toxic. I mean it's not normal to think I have to wait until my partner dies before something changes. I just got addicted to these chats. They reinforced my mindset, and allowed me to stay in the same toxic space.

It can become problematic when people often seek support outside their partnership when they feel misunderstood, unheard, or disconnected from their significant other. Fears of judgement, rejection or conflict may prevent open and honest communication with their partners, and they may look for empathy and understanding elsewhere. This external emotional support can inadvertently undermine the primary relationship.

In this case, my participant was revelling in negativity within a toxic friendship. It seems outlandish that someone would be willing to wait for the death of their partner to live a happy life, rather than working on the relationship, or deciding this person is not the one and moving on, but it's more common than you'd think. While this book's focus is on finding love and keeping it, not every relationship is made for the long term. Waiting for someone to die is no way to live!

Putting communication into practice

Humans are born to communicate—it's what sets us apart from the majority of other species on the planet. But this doesn't mean we always know how to do it; in many cases our communication skills are lacking. Key principles of good communication between partners include active listening (listening attentively and then reflecting back what you've understood your partner to be saying), cultivating empathy, expressing yourself authentically, being mindful of non-verbal cues, and prioritising relationship check-ins. If these things don't come naturally to you, think about getting assistance from an expert—for example, a qualified and experienced therapist or couples counsellor.

Importantly, put the phone down! Your online relationships are not actual relationships. We have a name for them: 'parasocial relationships'. Our deep obsession with these relationships means we risk alienation and disconnection not just from our romantic relationships, but more broadly. Put the phone down, and communicate with the person in front of you.

4

Once upon a time in love

The love we imagine

My own story

I met my partner twenty years ago at university. He was hanging about the cafeteria in the business faculty, and I was attracted to him instantly. He had dark hair and eyes, and typical Italian features, with a kind of '90s grunge vibe that made him almost impossible to resist. In a very typical rom-com way, our eyes met across the room and I felt a kind of sizzle: the energies of two attracted forces colliding. Perhaps I'd watched a few too many romantic comedies as a teenager, but I was quite sure that this guy and I were meant to connect.

Mobile phones were just hitting the market back then. I was carrying around a blue Sony Erickson, but I loved the old-fashioned idea of writing down my number for someone, not to mention amping up the drama a little. So I wrote my number down on a piece of paper, wandered up to him and handed it to him . . . and he called me. We went on a couple of dates, but there was really no connection there beyond physical attraction.

Some ten years later, when I was married and he was divorced and we were leading completely different lives, he found me on Facebook and sent me a friend request. I accepted, and we had a few random direct message chats. Another five years later, I was leafing through a book trying to find some writing inspiration. In my twenties I had the habit of writing notes inside books and on other things I collected along the way and tucked inside them: a train ticket, an old chocolate wrapper, etc. I'd gone through that book many times before. That day a number caught my attention, and a memory sprang to mind. It was his number. The first time he'd called me, I'd scrawled it down in the top left-hand corner of a page. I'd never noticed it there before. How strange. Was the universe sending me a message?

So I DM'd him on Facebook, and he responded. Weeks later we went on a date, and discovered that twenty years later our personalities did mesh . . . and months later, we were in love.

The power of storytelling

There's no getting around it—humans love stories. Throughout history, storytelling has been hugely important in human culture, from ancient oral traditions to modern day literature and media. We tell stories to help us understand the world around us and shape our own identities.

The US writer Joseph Campbell is known for his exploration of the hero's journey—a common type of story found in myths, legends and folklore across cultures. The hero's journey is about self-discovery, transformation and enlightenment; about finding meaning and purpose in our lives.

Stories also help us explore complex themes of morality,

justice and redemption, finding resonance in timeless narratives of good versus evil and the triumph of the human spirit.

Storytelling and love

There are certain storylines that resonate deeply with our fundamental hopes, fears and desires. One of these is the romance plot.

These stories offer more than mere entertainment; they serve as mental maps, guiding us through the complexities of human emotions and interactions, even when reality fails to conform to their patterns. At the heart of most romances is a timeless tale of love, desire and fulfilment. From classic literature to contemporary film and television, the romance captivates audiences with its promise of passion, intimacy and happily-ever-after.

Whether via the pages of a novel, on the silver screen, or through digital streaming platforms, romances give audiences a vicarious glimpse into the highs and lows of human connection. They affirm the universal longing for love and companionship.

Participants wanted a big story

For people to maintain a big love, they had to have a sense that *this was a big love*, and one of the signposts was that there was a story. But it had to be a particular *kind* of story, one in which they were the protagonist in a romance that was a transformative and transcendent experience.

Participants often found it hard to believe that such a big love could start on a dating app. Meeting online felt too strategic and premeditated. If participants had met online, they would often mention it as part of a larger story with more of a sense of destiny.

I was an actor for the majority of my life, and a bit of a vagabond. I travelled about from job to job and I was never really interested in settling down, finding a partner, having a family. I was more interested in having fun and really living life.

In my forties, I ended up in Spain, teaching English, and then my mum got sick—she had cancer and it was stage four. She wanted me to come home, so I did. I went back to Perth, and spent the next six months with here there, and it was beautiful. We just spent so much time talking and connecting. She was always disappointed that I never met anyone. She didn't just want me to settle down; she wanted me to find a big love. She said to me that she would send someone to me from the other side. I remember us laughing about it. I said, 'Mum, how am I going to know you've sent me this person?' And she said, 'You'll know. I'll make the signs very clear' . . .

When she passed, I was really lost. I didn't know what to do with myself. She was such an important part of my life, it just seemed impossible that she wasn't around anymore. I'd pick up the phone and think, I'll just call Mum, and then realise I couldn't call Mum because she was gone. It was always a shock.

I felt like she was with me, though, for a long time after she passed. Sometimes I'd turn around and just get a flash of her in the corridor, or I'd hear her voice as though she were speaking to me . . . Grief does strange things to you . . . but I don't know if it was grief, or what it was exactly.

After about six months I thought, I've got to get my life together, I need some sort of change, so I decided to move to Melbourne. I got a job as an acting teacher, and I reinvented myself, like I'd done so many times before. I had friends in Melbourne from my acting days so I wasn't lonely, and I've always been very independent.

At some point I thought I should start dating again. I'd had a lot of relationships, but they were never quite right. They were never 'the one', so to speak, and to be honest, I was okay with never quite finding 'the one'. It doesn't happen to everyone, and I tend to be one of those people who are content alone. Still, at some point you yearn for some sort of affection, physical and otherwise. So I got back on the dating apps and started meeting men. The quality was not great . . . not great at all, but I persevered.

One particular face kept coming around. He was on both Bumble and Tinder, and he kept popping up for me, but I just didn't find him attractive. And then one day, there he was again, and I heard my mum's voice: 'Stop here.' It was clear as a bell, like she was in the room with me—and I thought, Oh my god, this is my mum sending me the message she promised to send me.

So I swiped right and we matched, and he sent me a message very quickly. I won't lie, there was no chemistry in the chat. I persevered with it because I was quite sure Mum wanted me to meet this person. Eventually we met up, and instantly I liked him. He was quite different in person. In fact, I felt like I knew him for a lifetime—we were just in perfect sync with each other. On our second date, he came around to my house, and I made him a tea. When I put out the teapot, he reached across and rotated it three times . . . and I still remember, I just had goosebumps. I said, 'Why did you do that?' And he said, 'You've got to rotate the pot three times, otherwise it's bad luck' . . . My mum used to say that. She's the only person I know who did that—besides him now, obviously . . . and I just knew. I knew she'd sent him to me . . . We've been married for four years. He's my one.

Across the course of my research I heard a multitude of moving stories about love. This kind of big, iconic, transcendental story often signalled to people that this was the right person; to stick with it, but also to work at it. It meant they chose this person: they were resolute and as a result were willing to continue on even when times were tough.

Love and the imagination

When I told a friend of mine the story of how I met my partner, I said, 'If I met him now, without the backstory, I don't think I would have been interested.'

'What do you mean?' he asked.

'There's something about that story. There's a magic to it—and now I think there's a magic to him . . . but maybe it's just the story.'

'But does it matter?'

It was my turn to ask, 'What do you mean?'

'Well, does it matter if it's real or imagined? If that's how you feel, that's really the end of it.'

The words really hit me: did it matter if it was real or imagined? And he was right, it didn't matter. It turns out that the imagined elements of love are often as important as the tangible ones.

If you think about any one of your romances, you'll find that some of that love was constructed through your imagination. When you first met, you thought about who this person was, how your story together might play out. You fantasised about this person, tried to guess their next move.

The psychologist Carl Jung offers further insights into the importance of imagination in love. According to Jung, the human psyche contains archetypal symbols that are common across cultures and time periods. With respect to love, they manifest as idealised images of the beloved as having qualities that fulfil our deepest desires. Whether we're looking for the nurturing figure of the mother, the heroic quest of the lover, or the divine union of soulmates, these images shape our perceptions of love. It's one way we seek meaning and fulfilment in our romantic encounters.

There tends to be more imagination in play when love is new. As we come to know our partner intimately, and over time, we spend less time imagining them, and instead focus on the tangible and the real. We can come to think we know everything about this person.

In a long-term relationship, the journey of discovery between partners is ongoing, and the element of mystery is vital for maintaining intimacy and excitement. Despite years of shared experiences and deep familiarity, there are aspects of our partners that remain enigmatic, requiring imagination to fill in the gaps. This mystery serves to keep the relationship dynamic and continually evolving.

♥ Case study: Medhi

Love at first sight

I met my wife thirty years ago in India. It wasn't an arranged marriage, which was common back then. It was a love match. It was love at first sight. I remember seeing her across the room at a wedding, and I said to my brother, 'That's the woman I'm going to marry.' He laughed and said, 'That will never happen.' Because he was very attractive, and . . . I was more a skinny young man, not like the heroes in Bollywood movies. I said, 'You just watch.'

I tried to speak to her that night, but she wasn't particularly interested. I thought, no matter. I found out who she was through friends and family, and then I made contact with her. I started to send her letters . . . I thought, women like romance. What's more romantic than writing letters? And I started writing, and writing . . . I wrote some twenty letters without a response. But I was committed. I wanted to show her I would go to the ends of the earth to go on one date with her . . . And you know what? On the twenty-third letter she responded. See the power of persistence!

She had the most beautiful handwriting, and I thought, beautiful, like she is.

Eventually she met me, but in secret, because things were stricter back then. And wow . . . She was studying to be a doctor, and here I was, just a lowly engineer. But she had the kind of mind that I knew would keep me entertained and challenge me. I must have impressed her too, because after that, it was on.

Not long afterwards, I told my parents that we had to go and speak to her family, because I intended on marrying this girl. Of course, they were shocked. No one was more shocked than my brother, who didn't think a man of my appearance could win a girl like her over. But appearance means nothing in the face of romance and love.

We were married, and eventually we came to Australia. We have two grown-up sons now, and I think one day we will see them get married too.

What do I think kept us together?

I think she was the love of my life from the moment I saw her. But in addition, she's a smart woman, we challenge each other, and she's incredibly fun. She's the type of person who will suddenly suggest going rock climbing, or singing a song together, or wearing fun clothes. I don't think many people do those sorts of things—people tend to be boring. The one thing you can't be in a long-term relationship is boring . . . because everything is mundane. Life is mundane. The only way we make it special is by injecting the fun, the romance . . . It's us, we have to make it happen.

5

Physical touch and passion

How to sustain your love life

One of the things I worry about is sex. We don't have much sex
anymore . . . Sex was never our number one thing—I've had better
sex with other people—but this relationship was more than that;
there was chemistry and connection there. We've been monogamous for nine years, and that was a really important thing for us.
Loyalty and monogamy. But I worry as we move forward, about
sex—because there's just no interest there anymore . . . and I guess
that will just progressively get worse. I get hung up on it, I think
because when I was young, sex was a big part of my life . . . and I
guess now, in this second chapter of my life, it's not. It's a loss of
many things I guess: sex, and also youth, and who I was then.

The majority of participants in long-term relationships said
sex was an issue they often worried about. The majority also
listed it as something that needed to be nurtured and kept
alive. However, the participant quoted above made a broader

connection of the lack of sex with lost youth, plus the fear of getting older, of stagnancy. All of which can compromise our capacity or desire to remain in long-term relationships. Sex is not merely sex in this case, but a physical facet of a complex story between two people.

Erotic love, then and now

In Ancient Greece, erotic love was personified as Eros, a mischievous deity who wielded his bow and arrows to inspire love and desire in mortals and gods alike. Eros symbolised the irrational and uncontrollable nature of desire, capable of stirring passion and chaos in equal measure. The Romans identified Eros with their own god of love, Cupid. Throughout the Middle Ages and into the Renaissance, the concept of eros was transformed, as Christian theologians tried to reconcile the pagan idea of erotic love with Christian morality, emphasising virtues such as chastity and restraint. The troubadours of medieval France composed lyrical poems celebrating courtly love, an idealised form of eros that emphasised devotion, loyalty and spiritual longing.

Today, eros is stuck somewhere between the digital world and the physical, between imagination and reality, between power, politics and society.

Our modern obsession with sex

Here is an account from one woman in my research:

> One of the things I hate about dating is that men my age have a weird relationship with sex. It's like they all grew up watching porn and they either can't get hard if they're not watching porn, or they

have these weird fetishes. Half of the time you end up having sex with them while they're staring at their phone. No connection. Nothing. I mean, I get they can't perform in a real world environment and have unrealistic expectations of sex because of porn—at least, that's what my psychologist has told me—but at the same time, I can't help but feel less than. Like I can't have normal, connected, intimate sex [so] there must be something wrong with me.

And another:

I went to dinner with him and he was perfectly pleasant. A gentleman, in fact. We'd been on a couple of dates and there was a real attraction between the two of us. We ended up at his place. As soon as we started, you know, getting down to business, he turned into this other person, and he started saying the most disturbing things to me. Not just dirty talk, but things like, 'You're nothing. You're a waste of space. You don't deserve to be alive' . . . I said, 'Put your clothes on and get out.' Then he was apologetic and said he was just adopting a persona, and it was dirty talk. I said, 'That's not dirty talk—you're a sadist.' I kicked him out and blocked him. Where did this man get the idea that this is what women want to hear?

In modern society, the obsession with sex permeates virtually every aspect of our lives, from advertising and media to literature and entertainment. While human beings have always been fascinated by sex, the intensity of this obsession in contemporary culture is something new.

One key factor is the commodification of desire in consumer culture. In an increasingly consumer-driven society, sex sells, and advertisers capitalise on our primal instincts to market products and services. From fashion and beauty to food and automobiles, sexual imagery is used to entice consumers and create desire and longing. This constant bombardment of sexualised messages reinforces the notion that sex is not only desirable but also *essential for personal fulfilment and happiness.*

Advances in technology have revolutionised the way we consume and access sexual content. The internet, in particular, has made it much easier to access pornography and erotica, making sexual imagery and content more readily available than ever before. With just a few clicks, people can access a vast array of explicit material, catering to every imaginable preference and fetish. Many of my younger participants talked about feeling disconnected from physical sex, saying that watching porn from a young age had made it difficult to engage in sex with a partner. The expectations gleaned from a diet of porn were often unrealistic, debased women, and were disturbingly violent.

Some researchers believe that the widespread availability of internet pornography has led to a decrease in sexual activity in certain demographics, particularly younger adults. With easy access to an endless array of sexual content online, individuals may choose to satisfy their sexual desires on their own rather than seeking out intimate relationships.

The media plays a significant role in shaping our perceptions of sex and sexuality. From movies and television shows to music videos and social media, popular culture bombards us with idealised images of sex and romance. These often depict unrealistic standards of beauty, performance and pleasure, leading people to feel inadequate and insecure. The prevalence of sex in the media can also desensitise audiences to the *emotional and relational aspects of sexuality*, reducing it to a mere physical transaction. But It was the emotional and relations aspects of sexuality which were of particular interest to participants. They were interested in the way sex bound two people together; the way it made their partner, and themselves, feel; how to retain chemistry in a long-term relationship. Sex, for the majority of participants, was complex and something they considered deeply. Often they had a sense that they were alone in this kind of focus—that sex came easily and spontaneously to others.

As social beings, humans are hardwired to seek out and form intimate connections with others, and sex serves as a fundamental means of bonding and reproduction. Our desire for sex is deeply rooted in our evolutionary history, driven by biological urges and hormonal impulses that compel us to seek out sexual gratification.

Sex is often associated with power, status and identity. Some people seek validation through sexual conquests and experiences. For men, in a culture that equates sexual prowess with social success and desirability, the pressure to perform can be overwhelming. And women in my research often described frustrating gendered expectations. As one woman said:

> I was dating this nice guy, but he kept asking me how many men I'd slept with. I felt a sense of judgement, because I'd slept with a few guys. I mean, it was all in the context of long-term relationships—they just didn't work out. I found it odd, and a real turn-off.

It's important to critically examine society's ideas about sex if we want a more balanced and nuanced understanding of human sexuality—and a more fulfilling sex life ourselves.

Loss of passion over time

> We got to the point where we were fixated on the number of times we were having sex. Like, once a month is not enough. It has to be once a week. . . . And then it became almost scheduled in. Problem was, Tuesday would roll around and we knew it was time, and we

just had no desire for it, but we'd go through with it because we knew we had to . . . And it was awful.

Passion in relationships often begins with intense desire and excitement but diminishes as novelty fades and routine sets in. Initially, uncertainty and new experiences fuel passion, but over time, familiarity and daily obligations can create monotony, leading to a loss of ardour. As couples prioritise stability over risk-taking, complacency can arise, stifling the excitement and spontaneity necessary for sustaining passion.

Career demands and family responsibilities can also divert attention from the relationship, leading to emotional distance. Unresolved conflicts and unmet needs may inhibit passion, emphasising the importance of open communication and emotional reconnection to revive intimacy.

In the digital age, technology and social media can also distract from quality interactions, potentially causing jealousy and insecurity, and undermining trust. Setting boundaries around technology use and prioritising direct interaction can help maintain intimacy and passion.

In spite of these challenges, passion can be rekindled through effort and commitment to nurturing the relationship. By addressing issues, nurturing connections and reintroducing novelty, couples can rejuvenate their passion and enjoy a dynamic, lasting relationship.

A focus on numbers can be restrictive, as my participant found, but for some it allows for the conscious rekindling of desire. Remember, libidos change: one participant said they didn't have sex with their partner for over a year after they started taking antidepressants. After this hiatus, and with some good communication, they came back together sexually. There is no one way to rekindle desire.

Dispelling the myth that sex is easy

I've had sex with over 200 men. I went through a stage in my twenties after a bad break-up where I just wanted to get my mojo back. I felt like every relationship I got into, I became obsessed about the other person, and then if there was a break-up it ruined my sense of self-worth. I wanted to go back to just having a hook-up and moving on, no strings attached. It sounds counterintuitive—hooking up for self-worth—but it worked. I basically changed my profile on Tinder to 'here for a good time, not a long time', and lined up hook-ups, virtually every day. It was easy—I gave these guys instructions on when, where, how . . . and most of them did exactly as they were told. No issues. And then one day I felt like I could go back to actually looking for a relationship. The thing is the sex for hook-ups' sake is easy; it's transactional. It's sex in a relationship that's hard. It's the intimacy in a relationship that's hard.

This quote from a participant hit me, summarising the transactional nature of a hook-up versus the complexity of sex in an intimate relationship. Sexuality is a complex and deeply personal aspect of human experience, yet it is often portrayed in popular culture and media as something simple and effortless. This misconception leads many individuals to believe that sex is easy; that it should come naturally; that everyone else is having a more fulfilling and satisfying sexual experience than they are. However, this is a myth that can have damaging consequences for individuals and relationships, as it obscures the reality of sexual diversity, complexity and vulnerability.

The media and popular culture often glamorise and oversimplify sexual encounters, which can create unrealistic expectations and pressures, leading people to believe that their own experiences of sex should conform to these idealised depictions.

In many cultures, there is a stigma surrounding discussions of sex and sexuality, leading to a lack of open and honest communication about sexual desires, boundaries and experiences. This culture of silence and shame can make it difficult for people to seek support or guidance when navigating their own sexual relationships, leading to feelings of isolation and inadequacy.

The prevalence of hook-up culture and casual sex in contemporary society may contribute to the perception that sex is easy. In a culture that values instant gratification and superficial connections, there can be pressure to engage in sexual activity without emotional intimacy or meaningful communication. This can create a false sense of confidence and competence, as people may prioritise quantity over quality in their sexual experiences. Most of my participants indicated that the hook-up was easy: it was long-term intimacy which was hard.

The reality is that sex is anything but easy. It requires communication, trust, vulnerability and mutual respect between partners. Every individual is unique, with their own desires, boundaries and preferences, and navigating these complexities requires empathy, understanding and active consent. Sexual experiences can also be influenced by a wide range of factors including past traumas, body image issues, and cultural and religious beliefs.

Dispelling the myth of easy sex is crucial for better communication and greater authenticity in sexual relationships. Through acknowledging the complexities and vulnerabilities inherent in sex, people can bring compassion and understanding to their own sexual experiences and those of others. Open and honest communication about desires, boundaries and expectations is essential for building trust and intimacy in relationships, allowing partners to explore and navigate their sexualities in a safe and respectful manner.

By challenging the myth of easy sex, we can create a more inclusive and empowering culture that celebrates the diversity and complexity of human sexuality.

Sex is more than just sex

Sex is more than just sex. It's about all the other small things. Those kinds of physical intimacy which keep you connected. You know—walking into the kitchen and smacking your partner on the bottom. A playful kiss before work. Holding someone's hand during a movie . . . Those things are things that make you feel connected to that person.

Keeping the spark alive in a long-term relationship requires effort, communication, and a focus on intimacy and connection. While the initial passion of a new relationship may naturally fade over time, there are many ways to cultivate and sustain a fulfilling and satisfying sex life with your partner.

Prioritising intimacy outside of the bedroom is important for maintaining a healthy and satisfying sex life. Make time for regular date nights or quality time together, free from distractions or responsibilities. Do things that bring you closer as a couple, whether it's cooking a meal together, going for a hike, or simply cuddling on the couch and watching a movie. Building emotional intimacy and connection outside the bedroom can also enhance sexual intimacy and strengthen your bond as a couple. Don't underestimate the power of small gestures! Whether it's a tender kiss goodbye in the morning, a flirtatious text message during the day, or a passionate embrace before bed, small moments of connection can go a long way in maintaining intimacy and desire between you and your partner.

6

Create a relationship that's right for you

Don't just stick to the script

One of the things that keeps me out of a long-term relationship is I feel like I have to participate in this icky kind of story. You know . . . There's a way relationships have to be lived, and I don't want to be in that. I'm fifty years old—I've been married before, I've lived with partners, I have two girls in their late teens . . . I don't want a man just wandering around the house. I don't want to share a bed with a man. I like my bed and I like sleeping alone . . . I'm not saying that I don't want to have sex! I'm just saying . . . I don't want them in my way all the time. Maybe we could live in a duplex, side by side, and they could have their space and I'd have mine and then we'd come together for the fun things? . . . I've spent a long time living alone, I like my life as it is. The thing is, when I go on dates, they all want to move so fast, and combine our lives quickly, straight into this kind of relationship story that we have to live. I

want something else, something different . . . and I don't know if it's
out there.

Women in their fifties who were looking for love often said they didn't want to live with a partner, and that this was a barrier for them, because the men they dated expected to eventually move in together. Many of the women wanted a different type of relationship, but this seemed virtually impossible.

Research in Canada on dating among people over sixty-five showed that men in this age group often want and expect to eventually live with their partners while women prefer to maintain independent living arrangements.

So why is this the case?

Importantly, living in a long-term relationship with a man often entails a lot of labour for a woman, both seen and unseen. Beyond the conventional responsibilities women are expected to take on, like household chores, childcare and emotional support, there's often the unspoken burden of managing the intricacies of daily life. This labour includes the mental load of planning and organising, such as coordinating family schedules, remembering important dates and managing household finances. It can be exhausting and often goes unrecognised, leading to feelings of frustration on the woman's part, and imbalance within the relationship. It's unsurprising that many women would turn away from this dynamic, and be unwilling to return to such an arrangement.

What society expects

Participants in my research who were in long-term relationships often said that one of the key factors in keeping their relationship together was creating a relationship that worked for them, even if it deviated from what society expects.

From fairy tales and romantic comedies to popular music and literature, Western culture is saturated with idealised portrayals of love and romance. Love is typically depicted as passionate, all-consuming, and characterised by dramatic gestures of affection and devotion.

Add to that traditional gender roles, which often dictate rigid expectations about how men and women should behave in romantic relationships, and the related stereotypes about masculinity, femininity and power dynamics. While we might argue that such gender roles are antiquated, they were very much alive and well within my own research sample. Popular ideas about marriage and monogamy also create pressure for couples to behave in certain ways when it comes to commitment, fidelity and longevity in their relationships.

People can end up measuring their relationships against these unrealistic or rigid standards, and feeling insecure and inadequate.

The rise of social media and digital technology has magnified these pressures, adding a platform where people showcase prettied-up versions of their lives and relationships, so that viewers measure their own relationships against idealised images of happiness and romance.

If you want to be in a happy long-term relationship, you need to be prepared to ditch the script and find what works for you.

Finding what works for you

The majority of participants in my research who were in long-term relationships talked about the importance of finding their relationship's own particular shape. They gave examples of how their relationship varied from the basic script, from sleeping in different bedrooms, to opening up their relationship to different sexual partners, to creating particular bonding rituals, to living apart. The basic idea was that they'd found a way to live their relationship that made both parties happy.

> My partner and I have been together for close to twenty years. A while back we decided to open up our relationship to other sexual partners. This means if we want to have a hook-up, no strings attached, we're not going to deny each other the opportunity. But that's where it begins and ends—there are no feelings involved. The connection and intimacy is between my partner and I . . . I guess to some degree this kind of thing is perhaps more accepted in the queer community, because we didn't necessarily have a rule book for how to live relationships, so we can experiment more on what might work for us . . . I think there are some pretty pervasive rules around how to live a relationship as a heterosexual . . . but the world is shifting, people are changing. I think the only way to live a long-term relationship is to make up your own set of rules, and ignore what everyone else is saying. Every relationship is unique.

#RelationshipGoals

> So I've been dating this guy for a year and I've never posted him on my social media account . . . I just didn't feel comfortable with it—and I thought, if we break up, I'm going to have to delete the evidence . . . and it's just embarrassing. But then I noticed that a friend of mine posted on their Instagram account after a couple of months . . . a new relationship . . . declaring how much she was in love with him, and suddenly I started thinking, there's something wrong with our relationship. We started dating a year ago and we only just started to say I love you . . . Comparatively, it seems like we're moving at a snail's pace.

In the digital age, social media has become an integral part of how we navigate and experience relationships, influencing our perceptions, behaviours and expectations. Many people find themselves feeling inadequate or discontented when comparing their own relationships to those portrayed by others online, and envious of other couples' seeming happiness, success and compatibility.

The concepts of #RelationshipGoals and #CoupleGoals have become ubiquitous on social media, with users sharing images and anecdotes about seemingly perfect couples and relationships as inspiration or benchmarks for others. From extravagant vacations and romantic gestures to picture perfect moments and declarations of love, these stories and images set unrealistic standards and create pressure for couples to emulate them.

Social media also influences how relationships are announced to the world. The concept of 'soft launching' relationships involves gradually introducing a new partner to one's social media network, testing the waters and gauging reactions before making the relationship public. 'Hard launching' means making a more formal and public declaration of your relationship status, often accompanied by a carefully curated photo or announcement.

Many of my participants were afraid that things weren't happening fast enough, or on time—for example, 'We should have posted about our love story on social media sooner', or 'We should have moved in sooner.' There was a pace set that didn't allow for individual nuances, or the freedom to allow your own relationship to develop at the pace that suits you and your partner.

The expectations around straight relationships

Some of my participants raised interesting points about the expectations around heterosexual relationships in particular, and how stifling these expectations can be to relationships. Social media plays a significant part in perpetuating and reinforcing these ideas. From the moment people enter into a straight romantic relationship, they are bombarded with messages and images about how it should unfold, complete with milestones such as engagement, marriage, home ownership, pet ownership, and starting a family.

The concept of 'settling down' is central. This typically entails getting married, buying a house and starting a family, and is rooted in traditional ideas about success, stability and fulfilment, with marriage and home ownership as symbols of maturity, prosperity and social status. Social media platforms like Instagram, Facebook and Pinterest showcase images and stories of couples who have achieved these milestones, presenting a glossy, idealised version of domestic bliss that others aspire to emulate. Those whose relationships don't follow this pattern may feel like they're doing something wrong.

The pressure to conform is increased by our culture's emphasis on traditional gender roles. Men are typically expected to be the primary breadwinners and providers, while women are often expected to prioritise caregiving and domestic responsibilities. This reinforces specific ideas about what a successful relationship should look like.

The pursuit of these ideals can undermine the individuality and authenticity of heterosexual relationships, stifling creativity, spontaneity and personal growth. Couples may feel they have to prioritise meeting these milestones rather than paying attention to what they really want, leading to disillusionment and dissatisfaction.

Creativity is key to finding and living an original relationship that brings joy. Think big and think broad. Realise what's seen as the norm in our society may not work for you—and be open to finding out what does!

♥ Case study: Sam

When the fit isn't right, but you stick to the script

Sam is in his forties, he lives in Sydney and works in engineering. He's been married before, and now he's looking for love. I asked him about his first marriage. 'We were married in our twenties after a whirlwind romance. We'd probably been dating for six months before I proposed. At the time I thought it was the right relationship for me. It was just easy. There were no games, no big issues, no break-ups. It was just a kind of easy progression, and to me that felt right.

'I'd been in a couple of long-term relationships and they were often difficult, and then I'd dated for a while and it was a whole heap of games. So when I met her, I thought, this is it. Everyone around us was getting married, all of our friends, and it seemed like the right next step.

'My parents had been broken up for a really long time, since I was young, and they'd both remarried and divorced again. I didn't want to repeat the same mistakes. They were both single, alone, in debt, looking to sort out their lives as fifty year olds, and I just didn't want to be doing that. When I got to fifty I wanted to be set up, life-wise, and family-wise . . .

'So we got married, and we started on our journey together. We were living in Brisbane at the time. She was originally from Brisbane, and I'd moved up there for work, and that's where we'd met. We'd always talked about moving back to

Sydney, but at this point we were comfortable in Brisbane. We had great jobs, and we'd just bought a new house. Sydney just seemed a bit of a long-term dream.

'As the years passed, it became obvious that we were probably not such a great match. She was into the arts, and I was into tech, and we didn't really have much in common. We'd often fight. I felt like she started most of the fights.'

'What were the fights about?'

'I think she felt like her needs weren't being met. She wanted to be loved, a lot—and I didn't really know what she was looking for. I felt like I was doing enough, and so eventually it really felt like to me that she just wasn't happy with me—that I could never be enough. And those fights, they accumulated . . . We grew apart, even though we lived under the same roof. About five years in, we decided to have a baby. She was in her early thirties and I guess the moment had come for her to have a kid, and I thought, yeah, it was time too. We didn't really have sex that much anymore. We kind of went from having sex in the shower every morning to having sex once a month . . . if that. But we literally got pregnant the first time we tried . . . and then we virtually didn't sleep together for nine months. I felt uncomfortable about it and so did she—but I think it was a bit of an excuse . . . The desire had just disappeared.

'We had our little boy, and that's ironically when things really came apart. I was working a lot, and I guess she felt like I was never around to help, and it was just her and her family doing all the heavy lifting.

'We'd fight a lot—it was unbearable. We were struggling with the mortgage, on one wage, and the financial stress made everything a whole lot harder. And I started looking for jobs in Sydney.'

'Were you looking for an escape plan?'

'Yeah, on reflection, I was. I didn't tell her I was looking for work. It was a bit of a fantasy, really—and then I landed this job, and it felt amazing . . . I thought, I'm out.

'I told her I was going, full stop, whether she was coming or not. She was so shocked that I would make a plan without considering her and the baby, but yes, I guess I was just looking for an escape—and this was it.

'We got through it. We were very pragmatic in our conversations, and I guess we even talked about staying together just for the family.

'I moved to Sydney, and she followed me a couple of months later after she found work, and we struggled on for a couple of years. We even made a plan around scheduling in sex once a week, but it always felt so contrived, and I got the sense she wasn't interested at all.

'I don't think she was ever really in love with me . . . Maybe vice versa. We confused an easy start to the relationship with love.

'About three years into Sydney, she said she was leaving me, and . . . it wasn't dramatic; it was actually very amicable at the start. We moved out of our rental and decided on an arrangement of care for the baby, and that was it.

'We spent over a decade together and it all came to a bit of a nothing really . . .

'So now I have really turned into my parents. I'm looking for love again in my forties, and starting over again with everything.'

'Do you think the relationship could have been salvaged?'

'I don't think so. I don't think we were ever *that* person for each other. We just weren't a great fit. There was no big love between us—and we always just operated as individuals.'

7

The individual and the team

Collaboration is key

Where we found we really started to come unstuck was . . . we were acting too much like individuals rather than a team. We got to a point where it was just about me or about him, separately. We got stuck in the day-to-day of our lives, our personal ambitions, and we didn't leave any room for us. In fact, we got to the point where there was no us. I guess we didn't realise we had to be a team. It was only after we went to counselling that we realised we had to think like a team, or be more like a team. That doesn't mean we lost the individual. It just means the two coexist side by side.

My participants often expressed the idea that in a successful relationship, partners work as a team. Collaboration, cooperation and shared goals all tend to promote relationship satisfaction and longevity. The majority of my participants in long-term relationships reinforced the need to be part of a team, but also retain your individuality.

Teamwork throughout history

In many traditional societies, relationships were characterised by an emphasis on cooperation and interdependence. Families and communities relied on teamwork to fulfil essential tasks such as farming, hunting and raising children. Relationships were not solely viewed through the lens of individual fulfilment but seen as part of a larger collective, where mutual support and collaboration were essential for survival and prosperity.

The rise of capitalism and industrialisation in the West during the eighteenth and nineteenth centuries led to changes that reshaped relationships. With the growth of urbanisation and the emergence of wage labour, individuals increasingly defined themselves in relation to their own personal ambitions rather than their roles within their community. Enlightenment ideals further emphasised individual rights, freedom and autonomy.

The advent of modern psychology in the late nineteenth and early twentieth centuries also contributed to the emphasis on the individual. Psychologists such as Sigmund Freud and Carl Jung highlighted the importance of individual identity, desires and motivations. The rise of psychoanalysis and self-help movements promoted the idea of self-discovery and personal fulfilment as essential components of mental well-being. In the digital age, personal devices, social media platforms and online communities have enabled people to connect with others on their own terms, often prioritising their own needs over collective goals or responsibilities. The team is rarely celebrated.

While the focus on the individual has undoubtedly brought about advances in personal freedom and creativity, it has also led to challenges in the realm of relationships. The emphasis on self-fulfilment and personal autonomy can sometimes undermine the importance of teamwork, cooperation and mutual sacrifice within romantic partnerships. In a culture that celebrates individualism and independence, couples may struggle to balance their own desires and aspirations with the collaborative effort required to maintain a healthy and fulfilling relationship.

What being a team means

Teamwork in relationships means viewing the partnership as a collaborative effort, with both people working together towards shared goals, while navigating challenges and celebrating successes together.

When partners approach their relationship as a team, they are more likely to talk openly and honestly, and to work together to address conflicts and disagreements constructively. Open and honest communication lays the foundation for understanding each other's feelings, needs, desires and concerns. Both partners need to feel comfortable expressing themselves without fear of judgement or criticism. Active listening is also essential, as it demonstrates empathy and a willingness to fully understand each other's perspectives.

By sharing their perspectives, listening empathetically and finding solutions that work for both partners, couples can strengthen their bond and deepen trust and intimacy.

Teamwork in relationships creates a sense of partnership and solidarity, where both people feel supported, valued and respected. When partners collaborate on household tasks, financial decisions and parenting responsibilities, distributing the workload equitably, they show their commitment to each other's well-being and happiness. This shared sense of responsibility gives rise to a deeper connection and mutual appreciation.

On the other hand, when there is no teamwork the relationship can suffer.

I spent over fifteen years with my ex. We never got married, but we were in a committed relationship with two kids. I always wanted to have kids. I was in such a hurry to have them! But after I had them, things became problematic within the relationship. I always felt like I was carrying the majority of the load, and this was at the detriment of my career. I had to take time off, and go part-time, and then, if either of them were sick, I was just expected to drop everything to collect them. I felt like my career had to take a back seat, but his just kept moving forward . . . and there was resentment around that. It was like he just didn't think the childrearing element had anything to do with him, or was kind of an extra, rather than the centre stage stuff.

When the girls were old enough for me to get back into it, I threw myself into my career again, and started working really hard to cover ground. In addition, we didn't have family in Sydney, so when we went out, it was always separately. I went out with my friends, and then he did . . . and before you know it, we were leading separate lives. The intimacy dropped off completely . . . and I started sleeping with other men. Just hook-ups, that sort of thing.

For some reason I stayed in the relationship, maybe for the girls, but when they hit their late teens, I thought, it's time for me to live my own life—and we split . . . If I had to be honest with you, we were never a team per se. We were always just individuals, and progressively that got worse.

Many participants talked about previous relationships that had ended, or current relationships that were challenged, because of an unbalanced focus on the individual as opposed to a team dynamic. Many said that at a certain point in their lives—post children, in particular—they each became a single unit, focused on work, spending their spare time alone or with other friends, while becoming more disconnected from their partner.

Individualism versus collaboration

Personal autonomy, self-reliance and the pursuit of one's own goals and desires are important for independence and personal growth, but they can create barriers within a romantic relationship if they are consistently prioritised over collaboration and compromise. People who are driven by a strong sense of individualism may struggle to prioritise the needs and desires of their partner or family, leading to conflicts and misunderstandings. Resentment can build up over time if one party prioritises their own needs as opposed to those of the couple or family. In many cases, this seemed to become obvious when the couple had children.

In a relationship, teamwork includes a willingness to consider the feelings and perspectives of both partners, and to make decisions that benefit the partnership as a whole. When one person is focused only on their own aims, it can undermine this collaborative dynamic, leading to competition rather than cooperation.

So how do you foster collaboration? It involves listening, empathy and, ultimately, compromise.

I think my partner and I work well together because we understand the value of compromise. I know that my goals are not her goals, and vice versa. I can be a workaholic. I'm fully aware of it. So you have to be fully cognisant of what's going on. Sometimes things get unbalanced and you have to have an open conversation around it, and make those tiny adjustment—or big adjustments.

8

Kindness (again!)

The special sauce

My ex was very unkind to me on a daily basis. I'm not talking about anything violent or anything, just regularly rude, uncaring and unkind. We had been together for years, and I think progressively over the years they got worse. It was actually off-putting watching them be so kind to complete strangers, and then be continuously mean to me. I couldn't understand why they did that to me. It was one of the clinchers for me around our break-up . . . Then they basically chased after me, saying I was the love of their life and they couldn't live without me. I stood my ground . . . I'd endured a serious period of time living with someone who was basically mean to me. I couldn't help but think, what's wrong with you?

The quality that participants felt was crucially important in long-term relationships was kindness. There was a sense that over time kindness could break down, and be replaced by resentment, anger and lack of respect. When this happened, the relationship quickly disintegrated. Curiously, we often reserve kindness for strangers, but don't apply it to those we love. Instead, we bring the worst parts of ourselves to such relationships, simply because we can.

Why do we hurt the ones we love?

People often shape their behaviour, appearance and way of interacting to create a certain impression in others. In the early stages of a relationship, they may 'perform' an idealised version of themselves, aiming to attract and retain a partner's interest. This performance may be partly determined by social expectations around gender roles and relationship dynamics—for example, men might aim to appear strong and emotionally stoic, while women might emphasise nurturing and emotional support. Then, as relationships mature, partners may reveal less flattering behaviours.

It's an odd fact that people often treat strangers with respect and courtesy while showing resentment and anger towards those closest to them. There are a number of theories as to why. Social exchange theory says that people are polite to strangers so they'll be treated well themselves, and that they feel more free to behave badly with people they're close to because there's already a connection there, and fewer social constraints. Psychodynamic theory says that people project their own unresolved issues onto their close partners. Attachment theory highlights how early relationships with caregivers set patterns that can lead to negative interactions in adult relationships.

Should you treat your partner like a stranger, then?

People often ask us how we've been together for such a long time—twenty years is a long time by today's standards. Ironically, I think the secret to our success is the absence. [We both work] within the film industry. We've had moments where my partner has had to work abroad for long periods, or I've had to, and there's been an absence. I guess to some degree that person becomes a little unknown during that period of time. You know, when you return you wonder who is this person and you have to relearn them . . . And there's something to that relearning—it keeps things fresh and new and it means that you treat that person like a bit of a stranger . . . It preserves the kindness to some degree, and maintains the mystery.

Not everyone has to spend long periods of time away from their partner to preserve the kindness and mystery, but there is something to be said for this approach. While it may seem counterintuitive, it's worth exploring the dynamics at play.

In the initial stages of a relationship, people usually present their best selves, wanting to make a good impression and facilitate a smooth social interaction. This mutual respect and courtesy can create goodwill and positivity.

However, as a relationship progresses, the dynamics shift. Intimate partners get to know each other's vulnerabilities, quirks and flaws, and this can lead to an entitlement or familiarity that erodes respect and kindness. In the absence of the social constraints that regulate interactions with strangers, partners can feel free to express frustration, impatience or indifference.

By acting as if their long-term partner is a stranger, individuals can rekindle the sense of novelty and positivity that often characterise interactions with someone new. This entails consciously cultivating an attitude of politeness, empathy and consideration towards one's partner. By prioritising kindness and respect, couples can lessen the risk of complacency or contempt that can arise from prolonged familiarity.

When engaging with strangers, people often strive to understand their perspectives and respond with empathy, as they lack the shared history and context they have with loved ones. Adopting a similar mindset towards their partner allows them to foster deeper emotional connections and mutual understanding, strengthening the foundation of the relationship.

Over time, couples can fall into predictable patterns of behaviour, and this can diminish the novelty and excitement that initially drew them together. By approaching interactions with their partner with fresh eyes and curiosity, people can inject vitality and spontaneity into the relationship, reigniting the spark of romance and affection.

A warning, though: adopting this approach should not entail emotional detachment or disengagement from one's partner. Intimacy is built upon shared experiences, trust and vulnerability. It's essential to approach this strategy with mindfulness and sensitivity, ensuring that it complements rather than undermines the intimacy and authenticity of the relationship.

Maintaining a balance between familiarity and novelty is crucial in sustaining a healthy long-term relationship. Striking this balance requires open communication, mutual respect, and a willingness to embrace both the comfort of familiarity and the excitement of novelty within the relationship.

Some people are inherently kind . . . and others are not

My partner is a kind person. It's how he grew up. We've spent ten years together, and sometimes I think he's still performing, like he's still bringing his best person to the relationship, while I'm just the harbinger of all things negative. The thing is . . . he's not performing; that's just how he is. Maybe he grew up in a kinder family and he models that behaviour, or maybe that's just inherently him. He's kind . . . I'm not, and it's so much work being kind to someone I know so intimately, but I'm conscious that I've got to do it. To preserve the respect . . . I think, strangely, in acting kindly towards him, he also changes in my mind, [and I] feel kinder towards him.

Yes, some people are indeed naturally kinder than others; there is ample research to support this. Kindness—which you could define as being friendly, generous and considerate—varies among individuals due to many factors, including genetics, upbringing, personality traits and life experiences. But even if kindness isn't second nature to you, it doesn't mean you can't aim to be a kinder person, or bring a greater level of kindness to your relationship. The benefits are huge!

A final word on kindness

Be kind, already! Life is difficult enough, and the least we can do is make an attempt to be kind to the people who spend the greatest amount of time with us; who have chosen to share life's journey with us.

9

Breaking the rules

The power of transgression

I'm very much the repressed, Catholic schoolboy. I don't want to have a threesome with my partner and someone else . . . I don't want an open relationship . . . Monogamy is very important to me. But I admire . . . in fact, I love the idea that she's a rule-breaker. She does things that most people would think are too much. She'll walk around at Mardi Gras with her lingerie on, or have in-depth sexual conversations with people, or suddenly announce we should get a random tattoo on a Wednesday morning, when everyone's at work. I feel like I can explore my sexuality within reason, and feel like I'm breaking all types of rules.

Deep within many of us is a desire for rebellion, a yearning to be the maverick. From our childhood days, many of us aspired to be the ones who sat at the back of the class, boldly talking over the teacher or clandestinely etching marks into the desk. But for many, these acts of rebellion seemed reserved for those few who comfortably marched to the beat of their own drum, while the rest of us looked on, intrigued and captivated.

There is something undeniably mesmerising about a rule-breaker. Their steadfast dedication to living on their own terms creates a dynamic, magnetic energy. It's not simply the allure of the 'bad boy' or 'bad girl' that draws people in, but rather the potent, compelling nature of transgression itself.

In long-term relationships, this inclination to break the rules often lessens as people conform to societal expectations of relationships. This suppression of our wild side can lead to an existence that is not only frustrating, but drives people to seek transgression in other areas.

The secret lies in breaking the rules together.

Importantly, rule-breaking does not always have to be dramatic. It can be as subtle as opting out of any societal expectations that feel constraining. Such acts of defiance enrich our lives, adding excitement and authenticity.

Rule-breakers on the page and screen

Rule-breaking characters in books and movies have long captivated audiences with their defiance of social rules and their willingness to challenge the status quo. We admire their irreverence, and their capacity to be honest in an often dishonest world.

Han Solo, played by Harrison Ford in the Star Wars franchise, is a quintessential rule-breaker beloved by audiences for his roguish charm and rebellious spirit. As a smuggler and former Imperial pilot, Han is the archetypal anti-hero, navigating the galaxy on his own terms and defying authority at every turn. He represents freedom, independence, and a refusal to be constrained by the rules of the Galactic Empire or the Jedi Order. Audiences are drawn to his charisma and wit, as well as his unwavering loyalty to his friends. Han's eventual transformation into a hero willing to fight for the Rebel Alliance shows his underlying sense of justice and moral integrity, while his willingness to break the rules—whether out of self-interest or a desire to do what's right—makes him a timeless icon of rebellion and adventure.

Elizabeth Bennet, the protagonist of Jane Austen's classic novel *Pride and Prejudice,* is a spirited and independent-minded young woman who defies the constraints of Regency-era society in pursuit of love and self-determination. Unlike her sisters, who prioritise wealth and social status in their pursuit of marriage, Elizabeth values intelligence, wit and moral integrity in a potential partner, refusing to settle for a loveless union based on what society expects. Elizabeth's sharp wit, independent spirit and resilience in the face of adversity make her a beloved heroine. Despite the limitations imposed by her gender and social class, Elizabeth navigates the complexities of courtship with grace and integrity, challenging the prejudices and double standards of the society in which she lives. Her eventual love match with the proud and enigmatic Mr Darcy is a testament to the transformative power of love and the triumph of authenticity over social convention.

Han Solo and Elizabeth Bennet have captured the hearts and imaginations of audiences through their unwavering commitment to authenticity and self-determination. Whether navigating a galaxy far, far away or challenging the conventions of Regency-era England, these characters inspire us to question authority, embrace our individuality, and forge our own paths in the pursuit of love, truth and freedom.

Transgression in the bedroom

When it comes to maintaining desire in long-term relationships, some researchers argue that in pursuing stability, couples often sacrifice eroticism and excitement. The deliberate breaking of rules can reignite the spark between partners.

Transgression does not necessarily mean infidelity or betrayal; it can include anything from flirtation to exploring unshared fantasies, both of which can allow a renewed sense of connection. The anticipation of crossing societal or personal boundaries can heighten arousal and deepen the erotic connection between partners, adding a layer of intrigue and excitement to their interactions.

However, embracing these dynamics comes with inherent risks. It is crucial to establish open communication, trust and consent, particularly when navigating non-monogamous arrangements or exploring new boundaries.

And the rewards? By exploring the erotic potential of taboo behaviours, couples can create arrangements that fulfil both partners, while achieving a deeper understanding of each other and themselves—and thus a richer intimacy, passion and connection.

The many flavours of rebellion

Love is a deeply personal experience, shaped by individual desires, values and histories. What constitutes rule-breaking in love can differ greatly from one person to another. In other words, rule-breaking with regard to love is anything you want it to be.

As a society, we get hung up on sex, and so tend to think of rule-breaking in relationships as being about different types of sexual relationships or behaviours. But there are many rules, both explicit and implicit, that shape our romantic partnerships. You get to choose which rules work for you, and which you'd like to flout.

For some, rebellion may be about challenging traditional

relationship structures, such as monogamy, and embracing alternative models like open relationships or polyamory. For others, breaking the rules in the search for authenticity might mean simply not getting married, or not living together, or defying parental expectations in favour of what works for you, or navigating non-traditional family structures.

Rule-breaking in love can include rejecting restrictive gender roles. Men can embrace vulnerability and sensitivity, traditionally thought of as feminine, and women can assert more agency and independence in their relationships. This can foster more authentic and egalitarian connections.

For marginalised communities, such as LGBTIQ+ individuals or interracial couples, love itself can be inherently political, challenging discrimination and prejudice. Acts of defiance, whether through public displays of affection or forging relationships across cultural divides, can be powerful acts of resistance.

But it's important to acknowledge that not all forms of rule-breaking in love are inherently liberating or empowering. Some people want to break the rules simply because they're insecure or impulsive, or they do it with disregard for the well-being of others. Similarly, coercing or manipulating a partner under the guise of rebellion can perpetuate harm and undermine consent and autonomy.

Rule-breaking in relationships has the potential for both liberation and harm. It's essential that both parties know what's going on and agree to what's being discussed, and that decisions around rule-breaking are made thoughtfully and ethically.

What's in it for you?

It's worth considering how you could include a healthy dose of rule-breaking in your relationship. Embracing a spirit of rebellion can invigorate the bond between partners and infuse it with vitality and passion. By disrupting routines and exploring new horizons together, couples can cultivate a sense of adventure and excitement, and reaffirm their commitment to authenticity, growth and mutual respect.

In embracing rebellion within the confines of love, couples not only keep the love alive but can discover new depths of intimacy and joy in each other's company.

10

Fun

A vital ingredient

Fun is so important in a long-term relationship—having fun with your partner . . . because everything can be so boring . . . So much so that you seek excitement outside of . . . the relationship. It's important to rekindle that type of childlike joy and just enjoy each other's company . . . Laugh, do silly things, be kids again.

Why do we discount fun?

While love is celebrated as the cornerstone of a successful partnership, the role of fun within relationships is sometimes overlooked or undervalued. Yet fun is a vital ingredient in nurturing intimacy and connection, and maintaining the vitality of the relationship over time.

One reason why loving partners may feel compelled to sideline fun is our society's prioritising of productivity, responsibility and the pursuit of long-term goals over leisure and enjoyment.

People may feel pressure to prioritise work, household responsibilities and other obligations over recreation. We're told to save money so we can buy that house rather than going on that expensive but fun holiday abroad. And while there's an argument for both approaches, fun is often jettisoned faster than responsibility. The pursuit of fun can be perceived as frivolous or indulgent, so that partners prioritise practical concerns over the need for leisure and enjoyment.

Then there are the demands of everyday life—work, family obligations, financial concerns, and so on—which can create stress and tension within the relationship, leaving little time or energy for leisure pursuits. Partners may find themselves caught in a cycle of busyness and exhaustion, struggling to carve out time for fun and relaxation.

The fear of vulnerability and emotional intimacy can also contribute to an avoidance of fun. Engaging in fun activities often requires a willingness to be vulnerable, to let down one's guard, and to embrace spontaneity and playfulness. The vulnerability inherent in fun can be intimidating for people who equate seriousness and emotional restraint with maturity and responsibility. Partners may shy away from fun and lightheartedness, fearing that it may undermine their image of competence and maturity within the relationship.

The transition from the honeymoon phase to the realities of long-term commitment can also affect the amount of fun in a partnership. In the early stages of a relationship, the excitement of new love often leads partners to prioritise fun and adventure, seeking out novel experiences and shared activities to strengthen their bond. However, as the relationship progresses and partners settle into a routine, the intensity of fun and spontaneity may wane; fun may no longer seem to be a priority within the relationship.

Make fun a priority

Fun serves as a powerful antidote to stress, tension and monotony, giving partners an opportunity to reconnect, recharge and experience moments of joy and shared laughter together. By prioritising fun and carving out time for leisure and recreation, partners can strengthen their emotional bond, deepen their connection, and cultivate a vitality that enriches their partnership. Instead of treating fun as an afterthought or a luxury, loving partners can embrace it as an essential ingredient in a relationship that is fulfilling, dynamic, and resilient in the face of life's challenges.

In a long-term relationship, amidst the responsibilities, challenges and routines, fun often becomes a precious but overlooked commodity. Fun gives rise to playfulness and spontaneity, allowing partners to escape the pressures of adulthood and rediscover the joy of simply being together. Whether it's indulging in silliness, engaging in shared hobbies, or embarking on new adventures, moments of fun allow partners to let loose, embrace their inner child, and revel in life's simple pleasures. From impromptu dance parties in the living room to competitive board game nights, these experiences can create lasting memories and strengthen the emotional bond between partners.

Fun, intimacy and emotional connection

Fun is a powerful tool for fostering intimacy and emotional connection. Laughter creates camaraderie and a shared experience that deepens the sense of connection between partners. Through shared laughter and lighthearted banter, couples cultivate an atmosphere of warmth and affection, reinforcing their emotional bond and building a reservoir of positive memories to draw upon during challenging times.

♥ Case study: Emma

'We're not perfect, and that's perfect for us'

I was working in a gym at the time and needed to hire and train new staff. Management brought in a late hire, and I wasn't impressed because I'd already started the training schedule . . .

I can remember exactly where I was, the temperature, even that there was a storm outside, every tiny detail about my first conversation with her over the phone. I can remember the first time I saw her, as clear as day.

She fascinated me. I had to be around her; I was constantly trying to find reasons to be where she was. I'd go home and be so totally confused by how I felt. I couldn't name the feeling but it was strong. Unbeknown to me she felt the same.

I look back and think our attraction to each other was so powerful, unexpected and organic it just unravelled our lives, so we could make way for each other. Neither of us pursued the other. We just connected and grew into each other. We were drawn into each other's lives like magnets. The poems, the Hollywood romcoms and those sappy ballads are real. Chemistry, lust, longing, excitement, honest and pure—I wanted nothing but to love her. 'Drunk constantly' is the only way to truly describe it . . .

Compassionate compromise is what has kept us together across decades—being aware that people grow, and things shift to fit into the reality of that time of their life. Being honest with what you're experiencing . . . and not just as a partner, but a human. Everyone goes through stuff—death of loved ones, illness, changes in career, changes in social circles—and as a couple you have to find ways to navigate together, but also give yourself and your partner the security and space to experience it alone in [your] own way and time . . . Being proud of the progress [and] accomplishments of each other, not scared or jealous. We've always celebrated the wins, but give the credit where it's due. I'm not her shadow, nor is she mine. [We] talk, talk and talk some more . . . We laugh so much we act like silly teens on a sleepover. Stop being so serious! This is the person you're able to be silly with . . .

We get up and start again every day because time is passing and there's still so much to do. Twenty years together has taught us that we're okay with not being perfect. We've let go of unrealistic expectations of ourselves and each other. We're resilient individuals and it's this feeling of 'I'll be okay on my own' that gives us both an understanding of our commitment to our relationship. We're together not because we have to [be], or can't be bothered to leave . . . We're all in, out of love, desire, friendship, passion and connection.

A final word on love

Love's radical potential

This book and my earlier work explore and showcase the radical potential of love to bring joy, meaning and happiness into people's lives, whether it be romantic love, or love between family members or friends. Love is the only way forward, and we must commit to finding and nurturing it, and bringing to it the honesty, vulnerability and empathy needed to make it work.

Love, in its purest form, transcends the mundane and unveils the profound essence of human existence. It is not merely an emotion or a fleeting sentiment, but a force that disrupts the ordinary fabric of reality, revealing the inherent truths that lie dormant within us. While my research would indicate we yearn for romantic love, there are all kinds of love. Love between a mother and child; love between two friends; love between two perfect strangers. We're taught that there are lesser or greater loves, and that romantic love is at the apex, but there is no love pyramid. We can lead perfectly happy and realised lives with a different kind of love.

Love challenges us to venture beyond the confines of our individual selves, to embrace the other in all their complexity and mystery. It is in this encounter, this communion of souls, that we find solace, meaning and purpose. Love is the answer to the existential questions that plague humanity, offering a path towards authenticity, connection and transcendence.

Love urges us to defy the constraints of the status quo and embark on a journey of self-discovery and mutual under-standing. In the face of uncertainty and chaos, love stands as a beacon of hope, reminding us of our shared humanity and the boundless potential for transformation that resides within each of us.

Acknowledgments

I would like to express my profound gratitude to all the research participants—those who attended focus groups, engaged in interviews, journaled their experiences and completed surveys—and who approached this process with open minds and hearts. Their willingness to share the intimate details of their lives was invaluable. For many, this sharing proved to be cathartic; others felt that recounting their experiences of love and loss could ultimately assist someone else in their journey.

Several participants graciously reached out with follow-up messages, participated in subsequent research, and contributed to the Slow Love podcast series. I am deeply appreciative of their ongoing support.

I wish to acknowledge my supervisors at Western Sydney University, who embarked on a significant journey alongside me, and the University itself, which awarded me a scholarship to pursue this vital work. Although not all my research was conducted at Western Sydney University, my PhD served as the foundation and springboard for my future studies in this field.

I extend my heartfelt thanks to my publishers, particularly Juliet and Diana, for their unwavering belief in my work and for providing me with the opportunity to share it with a wider audience. Additionally, I would like to commend my editor, Tricia, for her exceptional efforts in bringing this book to life.

I am also immensely grateful to my partner's parents, Cathy and Pat, for their generous support in watching the children and assisting with various aspects of life. Their help has allowed me to fully dedicate myself to my research, writing and broader work.

Lastly, I am profoundly grateful to my partner, Gino, for his steadfast support and belief that my work would one day resonate with many. I also want to thank my wonderful children, Gigi and Pasquale, whose daily joy, humour and spirit continue to inspire me.

About the Author

Dr. Lisa Portolan is an academic and researcher based in Sydney. Her published works include *Love, Intimacy and Online Dating: How a Global Pandemic Redefined Romantic Relationships*, and she is a regular guest and contributor on Australian television and radio.

OPEN ROAD

INTEGRATED MEDIA

Find a full list of our authors and
titles at www.openroadmedia.com

FOLLOW US
@OpenRoadMedia